STARTING AND WINNING IN SMALL BUSINESS

Louis Mucciolo

ARCO PUBLISHING, INC.
NEW YORK

Published by Arco Publishing, Inc.
219 Park Avenue South, New York, N.Y. 10003

Library of Congress Cataloging in Publication Data

Mucciolo, Louis.
    Starting and winning in small business.

    1. Small business—Management.   I. Title.
HD62.7.M82   658'.022   81-12913
ISBN 0-668-05239-2   AACR2

Printed in the United States of America

Each is given a bag of tools,
A shapeless mass,
A book of rules;
And each must make,
Ere life is flown,
A stumbling block
Or a stepping stone.

R. L. Sharpe
(*Floruit*, 1890)

Dedication

To those intrepid entrepreneurs whose stories make
up the major portion of this book . . . their
willingness to pass on to others their own
"stumbling blocks and stepping stones." And,
especially for their initial determination and the
resultant sense of accomplishment they all feel.

To my own real life partner, Mary, whose nimble
fingers recorded it all . . . while, at the same time,
cheering for each of them as their entrepreneurial
progress unfolded.

CONTENTS

PREFACE: A FEW WORDS ABOUT WINNING

"Be prepared" is not the exclusive property of the Boy Scouts! In a very strong sense it's the battle cry of anyone striving for success in any venture.

That certainly includes anyone looking to win in his or her own small business.

Not too long ago I attended one of the many short-term adult evening courses offered by our local community college. The subject was "How To Start a Small Business." There were plenty of interested attendees and the professor was quite good, a person who had already been through the mill.

There were many highlights in that short course, but a few of them really stood out. One, a statistic, was a bit startling to all of us: "Out of approximately thirteen million businesses in the country, something over ten million are *small* businesses." Whether those figures are super-exact or not, there's a sparkling, exciting message there. What the numbers do say to those who take the time to listen, is that there must be one heck of a lot of winners among those ten million!

And that means something to you, the reader. For those of you who are interested in success, the field of small business is wide open, the target a giant one. There's plenty of room in the winner's circle, but keep in mind that only you and your own efforts will be *primary* to getting there.

Common Traits

There was another highlight in that course and it had to do with "commonality." It was easy to spot the students who could become winners, because of the similarity of traits that was evident in their makeups. By that I don't mean they were alike . . . far from it. A few were articulate and aggressive, others were quiet but, at the same time, acutely aware of whatever was going on around them. And they were in all stages of entrepreneurial activity . . . in fact, one standout had already failed in his first venture, but was furiously readying himself for another go at it.

The common characteristics that seemed to signal their probable future success were ones of *commitment* and *drive;* of *need* and *fulfillment.* There was an alertness, a willingness to explore ideas, a good sprinkling of common sense, and the extremely important attribute of perceptiveness. That ingredient helped to explain their grasp of the indefinable asset known as . . . a business sense. Additionally, all seemed fully aware that plenty of hard work and long hours were ahead, either with the books or on the job.

Preparation

It's not my intention to assume an academic stance atop some pedagogical lectern, to chart and outline all the possible do's and don'ts in this area. On one side, there's no questioning the benefits to be derived from knowing all the ground rules, researching the market, developing a program, and studying the business of small business. But, on the other side, there are the realities.

Most people who do start a small business do so with insufficient preparation and a lot of seat of the pants flying. Interestingly enough, though, there have been successes from both these schools of entrepreneurial endeavor. And, once again, that's a reality. In fact, most of the learning process in small business is acquired through on-the-job training.

Perhaps, for many, preparation before-the-fact might have made things easier and made success come a lot earlier . . . prevented a few failures, too!

Studying the fundamentals and reviewing what others have done creates awareness. In small business there are always surprises, and awareness helps you to meet those surprises, at least halfway!

Starting Out

In the many seminars and courses I have observed, the greatest interest seemed to center around the actual starting of a venture: how the initial die was cast, the events that governed the choice, the rationale of those beginner decisions, start-up capital, et cetera. This is why our interest centered around the newer ventures, especially their successful beginnings.

There are innumerable stories and case histories around about those who started on the "kitchen table" some ten or twenty years ago and who are now among our giant retailers or industrialists. Are these stories inspiring and instructive? Motivational . . . yes. Instructive . . . no. Not for those who are looking for some initial assurance and the specifics of starting.

Each of the book's interviews will be a totality, indicating the full spectrum of decision-making that took place during the startup of the individual business. Although all the steps of starting a small business are covered in every case, the reader should note that each of the interviews can be further evaluated to point up a different fundamental facet of entrepreneurship. Taken together, they help form a real-life primer of what it's all about in the often precarious "teach 'em by knocking 'em" small-business school that's outside the classroom.

In line with that, after each interview I have included some comments and observations. Here again, they will not be analyzed or measured against some real or imaginary standard. Instead, simply by re-identifying the positive moves, whether calculated or accidental, the observations can focus on the business sense of how each entrepreneur achieved the direction that may lead toward his or her goal.

Final Thought

They say you can learn more from failures than successes. Perhaps. But what I thought would be especially instructive was the very initial "how I started" commentaries of these new owner/managers. As you go through them, see if you can spot the commonalities that link them together, no matter their varied background or their particular enterprise.

Are they the touchstones that helped them to achieve a successful start? Do these characteristics relate to you? Can you cope with the oft-mentioned necessity of taking the risk? Do you have what it takes to win?

L.M.

INTRODUCTION

Why This Book?

In compiling my earlier book, *Small Business: Look Before You Leap,* I read and reviewed many of the small-business opportunity books. Most exhorted the reader to charge out and declare his or her financial independence . . . for example, *do it now . . . you can make it . . . look at these others who did . . .* Innumerable success examples ran through their pages, the warning flags of caution at rest. Plenty of good ideas were surface-explored, and talk of financial rewards, independence, doing your own thing, and super-positive attitudes tended to be the dominant highlight. In the minority were those books that concentrated on facts and information, providing no razz-ma-tazz, no overdone hoopla, and a lot more attention to red-flag warnings. My conclusion was that both types of books were useful and perhaps even necessary, because among those who start their own business, no two individuals are really alike.

But then, there was always the nagging question . . . what about all the present small-business owner/managers? Are the new entrepreneurs like the success stories in those books? Have their endeavors been fruitful? Would they give it up if they could? And, of equal importance, why did they want to become entrepreneurs in the first place?

Questions, questions—not necessarily arising out of any disbelief in the money-making opportunity books and their tales of the happy Tom T's, Laura L's, and Bob B's, but more in wonder of the *words* as opposed to the *realities.* The written words were usually the author's observations and conclusions and yes, on occasion, there may have been some fabrication of events. Not to deliberately mislead, but more likely to dramatize and illustrate a particular aspect of a small-business potential.

Separating the wheat from the chaff became my focus of attention. And my immediate interest was in the direction of the *modest* small business, the one that was started within the approximate initial financing range of $10,000 to $50,000 and which, if it became successful in a few years, was still run by the owner/manager and from one to ten employees.

This would include the retail store, the small manufacturing plant, the modest service business and the mail-order business, for instance. The conclusion of all this examination would lie in each small-business person's words—*their own words* to describe why they wanted their own business, how they managed to get start-up capital, how has it been going, and whether they are truly satisfied. Locale? Could be anywhere: all in one area, spread across the country, in the big cities, or around the corner from you.

Whom Are We Talking About?

This book relates to anyone and everyone . . . to you, the reader. That's because small businesses are started by anyone. We have interviewed entrepreneurs who never had a job before, both the recent college graduate and the formerly cloistered housewife, then there were those who have worked most of their lives, the retirees and the fed-up executives.

Add to that the mid-age group who wanted to control their own destinies or who were seduced by the attractions of a new and better life style. And don't forget the oft-labeled minorities: women, blacks, Indians, the handicapped, the Spanish-speaking, and others. Their entry into the small-business field is rapidly gaining momentum.

Okay, then . . . first they must have wanted to go into their own venture; then they must have physically done so; finally, they must still be in business—at whatever stage, beginning or established. It's this group with whom we wish to have a dialogue. For, as the *Business Failure Record* from Dun and Bradstreet points out: "Every year several hundred thousand firms are started, almost an equal number discontinued, and even more transfer ownership or control."

To the requirements already formulated for those we wanted to interview, another formidable specification was added, that of timing. Our interest here relates to those entrepreneurs who chose to start their small business during the turbulent later '70s . . . the era of the Vietnam aftermath, Watergate, stock market lows, recession, high unemployment, and sapping inflation. How did they fare through all or part of that? Wasn't it a risky time to start out? Is it a tough time now? Is there really any good or bad time to start out on your own?

There they are, those questions again. Thankfully, though, the owner/managers whom we will meet in the following chapters will tell us about their ventures, and while doing so, give us some of the answers to the questions that constantly surround the whole area of running your own small business.

What Are We Talking About?

The term "small business" means many different things to various groups of people. In bidding on government contracts for the military and certain other divisions, small business means companies with total gross sales of $24,000,000 or less in a three-year period.

To the Small Business Administration, the term signifies those businesses that achieve $1,000,000 or less in yearly sales for retailing or services or $5,000,000 or less in wholesale sales, a business that employs 250 employees or less in manufacturing. To most people, however, it means the smaller retail stores they frequent or the local contractor they employ.

Varied interpretations aside, what few people realize is that small business remains a dominant factor (at least numerically) in the nation's economic fabric. In communities, mid-size cities and metropolitan areas, they outnumber the large corporations, but in many areas they are even *more* meaningful than just numerous. For example, let's take a look at small business in the Big Apple, the nation's largest city, as excerpted from a Deputy Mayor's address in 1977:

> New York City's economy is based on small business and not the corporate giants that so often dominate the headlines. Of the 190,000 business establishments located in New York City, 98% are officially classified as "small business" . . . having less than 100 employees. Even more to the point, 90% of our firms have less than 20 employees each. It is the small business which provides the all-important entry-level jobs for so many of our residents who come from other parts of the nation—and the world—seeking opportunity for a better life.

Even the Dun & Bradstreet Reference Book, which lists some 3,000,000 businesses in this country, notes that 70% of them are worth less than $50,000 and only 5% are worth over $500,000. The statistics *for* small business are truly impressive.

But, unfortunately for many, the failure statistics are equally impressive—especially for those who jump in without sufficient preparation. In *The Business Failure Record,* published by Dun & Bradstreet, the categories of statistics cover a wide range and many of the conclusions are real eye-openers. Keep in mind that D & B is not reporting on the hundreds of thousands of businesses that may be discontinued every year. Their key relates to those companies who wound up in court as bankruptcies, or voluntary actions involving loss to creditors.

The greatest percentage of failures was attributed to "incompetence." High on the list were "lack of experience in the line," "lack of managerial experience," and "unbalanced experience." All together these four factors accounted for approximately 92% of the failures!

Additionally, the great majority of these failures occur during the initial two to five years of operation. In fact, the records show this to be true during every one of the past twenty-five years.

Let's hold it there for a few moments. It certainly isn't our intention to instruct you in failure. But these statistics can be meaningful to your success, even if only as a red flag waving a stop-and-take-a-look signal.

Although we would like to talk about success—and will do so—it won't freeze your hurry-up stride one bit to send for and study *The Business Failure Record.* It is revised annually; single copies are free of charge and can be obtained from 99 Church Street, New York, NY, 10007. Dun & Bradstreet also publishes a half dozen or so other pamphlet/booklets specifically for the small-business aspect of the nation's business.

That's it, then. In spite of the different labelings for small business and the extensive problems in keeping these ventures going, our case histories will remain in the category of the recently formed but still small business. They have some interesting stories to tell.

Who Needs A Small Business?

Many employees who would like to start their own business are reluctant to give up what they already have. They need those beautiful fringe benefits, which are so often available to the employees of the government and large corporations. Many of these same benefits can be found in the smaller companies, as well as in the union-intensive industries.

Forty-hour and less work weeks, pay for overtime, vacations, group insurance for life and health, retirement plans, sick leave, personal days, and, yes, even weather days. Then there are the steady income, the limited responsibility, and one more big one—the all important benefit of time! Time, after work, to be with the family, to go flat-out for sports and hobbies, to become involved in community affairs, and to relate to all sorts of personal pleasures and interests.

Hey, wait a minute, what about the other side? There are also plenty of negatives that employees complain about in working for someone else. There are the dead-end jobs, the questionable job security, the lack of independence, the politics, supervisory ego-trips, and more. Your ideas are often squelched or stolen, communications are only one-way, structured routines and systems are monotonous; there are the constant impersonal touches, the lack of identity, the lack of return for your contributions.

But, after weighing all the pros and cons, the employee aspect may still get the nod when you consider that in the large majority of cases, both the work and the responsibility cease the moment you leave the employer's premises. Unlike the entrepreneur and his all-encompassing entanglements, an employee is usually free of a total commitment to the job.

Of course, those employee negatives always assume an even greater degree of frustration when seen through the eyes of someone who is looking forward to starting his own small business. Instead, his new entrepreneurial outlook envisions the fabulous positives . . . the opportunity to do things his way, to control and use his own ideas, to taste the sense of independence, and govern his own energies; to potentially achieve greater financial returns, greater security and, in a nutshell, to be his or her own boss with all the rewards that this implies.

Admittedly, those are the truisms of succeeding in your own venture. But there are a number of not-so-positive realities, too. Almost without exception, you will as your own boss be working longer hours than ever before. Suddenly you have customers whom you must satisfy, and this holds true whether you are manufacturing, wholesaling, retailing, or supplying services. Needs and regulations start to spring up around you—legal, insurance, and accounting requirements, as well as those from local and federal government agencies. The realization sneaks up that maybe, in real fact, you are not entirely your own boss. At least not in the sense of being completely free to do whatever you wish.

You will have to respond, in one way or another, to your creditors and your competitors. Record keeping now becomes mandatory . . . for all sorts of standards, regulations, and the various taxing authorities. Employees, the landlord, suppliers, and a host of others are now a part of your responsibility . . . with other areas your total responsibility, such as product selections, advertising, profitability, finance, and general business direction. And, with all of that, you may in no way be earning, in the first few years, what you previously earned in much less work-time.

Is the whole thing worth it? Are you really independent? Should you make the attempt? Who needs a small business?

There we go, stumbling up against those questions again. This time, starting with the next chapter, we will be getting a line on some of the relevant answers from a real-life group of new, risk-taking entrepreneurs.

1 Are You the Type?

Richard Oakley, 34, and his wife, Judy, live in a comfortable home that requires no commutation to their small business.

Their sphere of responsibility is a small one . . . in fact, they can handle all their business within an area of not more than two-hundred feet in any direction.

But there's a penalty for this convenience, too. Every day . . . weekday, weekend, or holiday . . . is a work day.

They operate a service business that requires the constant presence of either one or the other . . . oftentimes both!

SIERRA MOTEL *
PRESCOTT, ARIZONA

We stopped off for a few days at the Sierra Motel to enjoy some rest and sunbathing by the poolside. The Oakleys had just purchased the business and were busy sprucing up the premises and confidently orienting themselves to the whole, new, and exciting idea of entrepreneurship . . . doing their own thing! One year later, when I decided to research this book, they were a natural for an interview.

Dick, I know this is the first time you've owned your own business. How did it all come about?

Well, it started with some kind of dissatisfaction with what I was doing, I guess. After college I went right to work for the airlines in Phoenix. In the beginning you had certain autonomy to do what you felt best. You had to work within a corporate framework, yes, but you could use your own good common sense to make decisions. By the time I left . . . after eight years

1

. . . that didn't exist and there were a lot of other things that started to get in the way.

Maybe it took that time for me to wake up, to understand what was inside of me all along. I've always been an achiever and I felt that any company should be result-oriented. Then, provided a man achieves the results or surpasses the results expected of him, the company ought to give him the support he needs to function.

After a while everything was by the book. You had to turn to the regulations to get an outline as to how you do your own job. That's kind of funny when you remember that the airline business was founded by some pretty gung-ho guys . . . people like C. R. Smith of American, Juan Trippe of Pan Am . . . people hell-bent for other guys and what *they* thought.

> *Going it alone looked a lot better than being the "organization man." Did Judy agree? To the idea of leaving a steady income and starting a business?*

Fortunately, yes. It's the kind of a move where it's important that your wife gives support and cooperation. She felt some of the things I did about the company and she knew me . . . the me that likes to get things done.

She understood that she might see less of me. But we ended up buying the motel, so the situation reversed itself. We really see too much of each other now, probably. Of course, our five-year-old daughter gets to see her dad a lot more than most other kids do . . . and that may be good, too.

Also, we wanted to move to a smaller place than Phoenix. We realized we wanted to stay in Arizona, so we took a look at a lot of small towns up north and finally set our sights on Prescott.

> *What finalized Prescott for you? Did you do some marketing research, or know that a business was available there?*

No, nothing like that. We did have a list of criteria that we thought was important in any relocation. That included the quality of schools, type of community, kinds of activities available. Climate was certainly an important criterion; we'd been used to Phoenix . . . hot, hot, hot . . . Judy and

I had both grown up in Illinois. We wanted to see some trees now, rather than all that flat desert. Maybe a different lifestyle . . . simple little things, in an effort to get back to our roots, so to speak. But close to Phoenix because our many friends and Judy's mother are there.

We wanted a certain amount of life and vitality in a community. We didn't want to get into a Sun City situation . . . where the makeup of the community is based on age groups and that type of thing.

I wanted some arts-and-crafts people . . . for the culture. But not an over-abundance of that. I think the mainstream or solid-core citizen is more down the middle.

How did you approach the idea of a business in Prescott? Start from scratch or buy one?

I did feel that buying one was more important than starting one . . . particularly in a small town, because small towns can be cruel to new businesses. You know, there's always a wait-and-see attitude. The towns-people will sit back and make sure the guy is legitimate and loyal to the town in a certain respect, and they won't really patronize him for a year or year and a half.

We ran into that attitude strongly in Sedona, which was a town of 6,000 or 7,000 people. We talked to various business people up there and that's one of the things they all said: "Boy, you'd better be prepared. If you're going to start a new business, you'd better be ready for a year and a half to two years of very little business from the community itself." That's something to think about, and it's not in the textbooks either.

After selecting Prescott, we began to make weekend trips up there looking for something to buy. I'd say we spent five or six weekends looking around. My background in college was a very general one, so we had no specific skill or commercial experience that would lead us into looking for any particular line of business. We looked at anything available, from liquor stores to kid's nurseries . . . we didn't know.

And, funny thing, one night we had to stay here, in *this* motel. I asked the desk clerk if she knew of anything in town that might be up for sale. She said, "Well, just a minute," and she left for the back office. When she came back to the front desk again, she said, "This motel may be."

There it is . . . ask a casual question and pick up a bombshell answer. I'd bet that a motel was a business you had never even thought about.

You're right, it never entered my mind. But what I've always tried to do is take advantage of the things right around me. You know, see the things that are right there in front of you. I remember a kid who used to get into those pickup baseball games with the grown men on Sunday mornings. When he realized everyone was always thirsty, he quit playing in the games and got busy selling Kool-Aid to his former teammates.

I think like that . . . making the most of things is a habit of mind you develop . . . it's kind of a mental scan of your immediate vicinity, to see if there's anything that can help your own ideas.

About the motel . . . it started to make more and more sense, the more we thought about it. We didn't turn around the next day and buy it. There was a month or more of thinking about it, and then negotiating, but the sense that it did make was that we weren't starting a new business; we weren't strictly dependent upon the people in a small town . . . who, as I said earlier, could be very cruel. We were dependent upon the traveler coming through from California, not knowing who's new in the small town. So it made excellent sense to buy a motel. And my background with the airline is travel oriented, service oriented, and so is the motel business.

There were twenty units in all. But we also had another consideration . . . there would be room to expand the motel's capacity. There was about 20,000 square feet on the other side of the present units and that was also part of the deal.

It all sounds like a heavy investment . . . the kind most beginners choke on.

No question about it. But let's take it one step at a time, the way we did.

First, there was a definite advantage to the whole motel idea, the fact of an assumable mortgage. You see, I had already quit my job with the airline. I wasn't working at all, and I knew I had no weight at all to walk into a bank and originate any kind of new loan.

It always seemed funny to me that somebody, let's say from New York, could walk into Phoenix and buy a $200,000 home on Camelback Mountain and not have a job. The buyer just assumes the existing mortgage. And, at that time, and up until a few years ago, there was no qualifying! You didn't have to walk into First National where the loan existed and say, "I'm John Doe. I make $30,000 a year and I spend $100 a month for utilities, and I've got a car payment of so much, et cetera."

The nice thing about the motel mortgage was that it was all assumable. No qualifying necessary.

There was a down payment . . . did you have that or was some special loan involved? And what was the purchase price?

The total package price was $262,000, with an initial payment of $50,000. I did have to take a partner into the deal . . . Jim, my good friend I went to college with. We both worked for the airlines for a while and I had sounded him out from time to time about going into business. This time I gave him a call and said, "Hey, how about buying a motel with me?" and he said, "Sure."

Again, this has to do with relating to what's around you. And that can very well be a person you know. A lot of people have relationships with other people that could lead to getting start-up capital for a business . . . but they're shy, they feel it could bust up the relationship. Well, why not take a chance and ask? If the friendship is that easily busted, it's not worth much to start with, and if the person does lend the money, then you're miles ahead.

Incidentally, the story of getting my $25,000 is an interesting one, too. Many times companies and corporations tend to keep the carrot slightly in front of your nose. If they know it takes you $12,000 to live, they'll pay you $12,500 or 12,750 or whatever, so it's very difficult to try to get money ahead. So, I started building homes in Phoenix on the side. I'd work four to midnight at the airlines, and get up at six in the morning and go out and build a house for three months, then turn around and sell it.

After doing that for a number of years, I went ahead and got my contractor's license. It takes three years of fairly hard-core contracting experience to get licensed and bonded, and do all the necessary things for the state of Arizona.

> *OK, $50,000 down and assume the existing mortgage.*
> *Did you work with an accountant first to determine the*
> *real value . . . the profitability factor . . . the ability*
> *to handle the mortgage? Or did you do all this yourself?*

No. In small towns, there are a lot of "Ma and Pa" organizations. They tend *not* to keep good books, they tend not to know where they stand. The motel was not really run like a business. It was just like a family living there . . . They'd take in $18 for a room and if they needed $18 worth of groceries, they'd take it out and go buy the groceries.

Sure, we hired an accountant, a CPA to come up from Phoenix and go over all the books. Unfortunately, his assessment was not something we could place complete faith in because the book work was so shabby. So we also reviewed the potential and the initial steps that had to be taken.

> *At least you called in a professional before you closed a*
> *deal. But how did you determine the value? Did your*
> *real-estate experience help?*

I guess the final determination to buy or not to buy was made on a sort of gut feeling . . . that the motel itself could be substantially improved and the rates increased by enough to allow us to do the necessary improvements. Also, that the assumable mortgages, which were at 6%, really could be handled . . . and that we could make money. Besides that, there were things that may have been sloughed off before . . . 24-hour phone service, longer check-in hours, the pool . . . things we could pick up on.

It was just that we had no real idea of the worth of the motel. In the beginning I was thinking, "Oh, my God, that's over a quarter of a million dollars." That can really scare the small guy. But it no longer scares me, and really, a quarter of a million is not much at all in this day and age for a piece of real property. What's important is that we knew we were buying a piece of real property; if worse comes to worse, you can always sell real property.

You try to think it out . . . add up the pros and cons. If you buy ABC Liquors, for example, you're buying nothing but inventory and a liquor license, and your good will or blue sky or whatever you choose to call it. When push comes to shove, and you have a problem, what do you really have to sell? You have no building; you have no land; you have no nothing. From a real-estate standpoint, the final determination to buy was based on, "We can improve this place; we can get the rate schedule working where it ought to be; the payments are reasonable; we have real property we're dealing with, and we know . . . I know, that real property tends to go up 5% to 8% to 12%, depending on what area you're in." We were comfortable with that.

> *I guess Judy understood, as you did, that it would take two to run it. Jim, your financial partner, was really a silent investor. What did you and he agree on?*

Yes, that's exactly the way it had to be laid out. We felt we needed $1,000 a month, specifically, to live at a certain level. The agreement between Jim and myself was that Judy and I would draw $1,000 a month salary and anything the motel made over and above that and the running expense would be split 50–50. Of course, we did have an apartment on the premises, too.

> *When you finally got into running the motel, did you start studying more about the business? Did you sharpen your maintenance skills?*

You can bet on that! The biggest thing I wanted to resolve in my own mind was, "Did I get a good buy?" So I talked to five or six motel brokers that deal specifically with motels in the southwest. I also read and have been reading the motel trade magazines and that kind of thing. All agreed that the relationship between the annual gross and the sales price was the thing to watch. A smart motel buyer should not pay more than four to four-and-a-half times the annual gross for motel property. There was no way to tell what the previous owner had grossed. But we've now been here one year, almost exactly. Based on *our* records, this motel is now worth $450,000 . . . and I have the book work, the facts and figures to prove that!

You mentioned maintenance. I have a definite feeling about that kind of stuff. My time is too valuable to do those needed chores. Why should I be out mowing this patch of grass, when I can pay some youngster $2 to do it, creating another job and cash flow in the community? Why should I be doing that, when somebody's coming into the office wanting five or six rooms, or who wants to negotiate a long-term rental while waiting for a house to close or to be built? It's conceivable that I could miss out on business if I'm immersed in a repair. I think too often we try to do too many things, particularly in the motel business.

I guess you *can* make money if you did all the work yourself, and your wife did the maid work, but we don't do it that way. We don't do any physical work around here. There's plenty to handle with supplies, services, supervision, the ongoing improvements, the longer-term rentals, and planning for the future. Don't forget the daily check-ins and -outs, credit charges, that take up a good bit of our time.

Planning is a magic word in the small-business field. Is the motel just a stepping stone? Now that the first year is done, what next?

I'm involved in quite a few things up here. First of all, my major objective . . . I have proven that I was able to meet the challenge on my own and make it. For one year the return on the investment dollar has been extremely good to me and my partner. I paid $8,000 to each of us last year over and above the salary I drew. So we're making 32% on our investment and that situation is going to get better and better and better.

In addition to the excellent return we're receiving, we now have a motel that is worth about $450,000. We paid $262,000 and we owe $200,000 on it, so we have a $250,000 asset sitting here. This situation has turned out to be a pretty solid one.

Our next objective is to move out of here, get a manager. A motel of 15–20–25 units is a marginal situation in terms of whether or not one can live someplace else and have a manager, and be able to pay a salary to a manager. Over the last year we've proved we can do that. Quite comfortably. So Judy and I will be moving in a short period of time, and that will solve, really, a big problem for us. We can now start enjoying some of the things we came here to enjoy. We've only had a handful of days off, and we work 24 hours a day, and it's confining. There's no question about it.

We have joined the Chamber of Commerce. We're not extremely active in it, since we are tied down and busy all the time. So, one of the basic reasons we're in Prescott . . . are things that . . . funny enough, we haven't enjoyed. I mean, we came to a small town so we could participate in community activities, and here we are, strapped to the wall in the motel. But one must pay dues. I'm a strong believer in that.

Last night we had a modest dinner in a restaurant across the way. It was a surprise to discover that you and your partner were the owners. How did that all come about?

Jim and I go together on that. All summer long people and families that we cater to in the motel business would say, "Where can we eat for a reasonable amount of money, in a nice clean place?" And that's one of the things lacking in Prescott; you have a lot of "Ma and Pa" cafes, a few really good places and you may have a Sambo's . . . but that's on the other side of town. A clean, well-run, family restaurant was needed here. These people can't afford to spend $45–$60 for a family of four to eat at a steak house. So we purchased the building across the street and remodeled it. I have a construction license, so I handled the construction. I ran back and forth across the street all summer long, making sure everything was done. I acted as my own contractor, which really paid off, because remodeling the restaurant, or handling the restaurant work calls for a license-bonded contractor. You can't just take a permit out as John Doe. So that saved a considerable amount of money.

We have a real nice facility over there, a real nice building. There's 3,300 square feet of Business-A property, which we bought for $90,000, only $27–$28 a square foot. There's nowhere in this town that you can buy a Business-A structure for under $45 per square foot, so we knew we were into that one right.

I guess we're talking another real estate deal . . . low down payment and assumable mortgage, right? That's also where your motel profits got sidetracked, furniture and fixtures, et cetera?

Yes, that's right, and the real estate financing of the restaurant was all assumable. Of course, there was a small down payment. Nobody's going to finance restaurants, specifically because they're a dangerous situation. I knew that, getting into it, particularly since we opened at exactly the wrong time. We opened in November, which we knew would lead us into five dreary, marginal months. Even if you open at a good time . . . well, you know the reputation of restaurants. Even if you do everything right, you lose money for six months.

There's a second floor there. Are you going to expand the present one or were you thinking of building another restaurant, with different food?

It may very well be a different kind of restaurant. I don't want to get into this $11.95 for veal parmigiana, or whatever. It seems to me that if a guy comes into a restaurant and looks at a menu that starts at $10.95 to $20.00, that service better be damned good. There's no room to allow for an inexperienced waitress, or something else that just doesn't go right. I don't really want to get into that kind of category. You can eat in my restaurant, look at the menu for $4 or $5 for a modest dinner meal and have a glass of wine with it, and if the waitress doesn't quite do everything right, you can almost justify it. You can say, "Well, what the heck, that was still a very good meal."

No, I guess we haven't quite decided what to do with the second floor in the restaurant. We've got a gentleman, who's living in Scottsdale during the winter months . . . he's done a lot of quality, fine foods restaurants, in the way of design work. He came up a couple of weeks ago, and he's got the floor plan to the facility, so we'll be expanding up there, but we don't yet know just what kind.

Dick, it's obvious that you haven't accomplished all this just by wishful thinking. Maybe you didn't originally start out with a business plan, marketing research, and demographics, but it seems to me that along the way you added a tremendous commitment, some sound thinking, and certainly a willingness to risk it. How do you feel now . . . was it worth it?

I'm generally very pleased with what we've done and what we've accomplished. It takes a lot of guts to get out and get off the dime like this. I see it every day. Nineteen out of twenty people that check into our motel want to live here, and I sort of laugh up my sleeve, because I know they can't or won't make the commitment. If somebody's going to hand them something on a silver platter in Prescott . . . yes, they'd move here and they'd live here and they'd sell their home in Phoenix or wherever. But 99 times out of 100, they just don't have the guts to really get out and do something. So they're going to go back home and they're going to live all their lives someplace that doesn't necessarily make them happiest.

Out of all those years . . . eight years with the airlines . . . I can tell you that my financial situation has improved six fold in the last 18 months!! And our living situation, living in a small town, has been wonderful for all of us.

Update

I revisited Dick Oakley because there were some things he had been contemplating that may or may not have worked out as planned, and I was curious.

Dick, did you ever get a manager for the motel and did you build another restaurant?

Yes, we now have a wonderful couple handling the motel area. But I must also confess to being dead wrong in the way I approached it. First, I created a profile of the person that would suit me . . . something like an ex-military man, one who looked good and was very personable. Someone disciplined and with some sales ability . . . that's what our business is all about. Preferably a husband-wife team with no children.

I put an ad in the paper, saw a number of people. Lo and behold, one day in walked my "profile." Ex-military, still with a flat top, very personable, and both he and his wife very neatly dressed. They came into my life the end of March last year and, to put it bluntly, they were crooks!

Knowing what I know now, they must have made a game of hitting small towns and small motels. They figure an absentee owner would not always be aware of the exact number of rooms rented and what comes in over the counter. As it turned out, they left in the middle of the night in a U-Haul. Over the next six months they charged about $15,000 to my Master Charge card, always being smart enough to keep their purchases below $50. They were caught in Texas after that. Boy, was I wrong!

That's why you can't beat on-the-job training. Tell me about the restaurant and any other changes since my last visit.

You're in for *another* story there. We sold the restaurant about the time the other thing happened. Guess that's why I wasn't checking the motel carefully.

The Juniper House was doing fairly well by this time and one of my guests asked if I knew of a small restaurant like it that was sale in Prescott. I said no . . . not then, anyhow.

A few days later, however, my manager and head chef (husband and wife) walked in to give two weeks notice. In small business, that can be very rough, trying to replace *good people* with their equivalent. I suddenly realized that there were 30 employees in that small restaurant. Multi-shifts because of our hours, six AM to ten PM, and the two days off rotation. It also dawned on me that I really didn't want to cope with that situation anymore.

That makes a lot of sense, providing the economics factor works out. The amount of effort versus the degree of return is a ration that tells the story.

You're right. That's why I looked in my registration files, found the name of that guest, and called him in California. It really wasn't necessary to sell but we agreed that if he could meet my terms, then it was possible. After everything was straightened out, we sold the business for $50,000 plus a five-year lease on the premises for $3,000 a month rent. Now I'm a landlord. We still own the building and the land. That ratio you mentioned works . . . the rent without all the headaches is not too far off what we were making in the restaurant.

That's terrific . . . and the funny part is the way your buyer found the restaurant was the same way you discovered the motel. Incidentally, how did the motel make out in its second year?

Great! The first year my partner and myself shared $16,000 total. Gross receipts then were $92,000. The second year our gross jumped up to $122,000 and we related to a $24,000 total. That's after both the managerial expense and an increase in my own salary.

Are you still spending much time at the motel? Without the restaurant, I guess the old 16 hours a day routine no longer exists.

There's more time to plan, true. I do relate to the motel every day and there's more to come. One of the original assets to the purchase of the motel was that extra 20,000 square feet of land available for expansion. This October an additional 10 new units will be constructed, making this a 30-unit motel. It will still be a small motel, but you have to keep abreast of the times and plan ahead.

Will the expansion pay off? Do you have the confidence that it's the right move at this time?

We're not talking about guesswork anymore. This is where *experience* becomes meaningful. My projections are usually a good deal ahead and I now have the monthly anticipated occupancy rate down to a pretty good science. Six months ago I projected last month's occupancy at 78% for $10,676 . . . I missed by one dollar!

Our business is comprised of 62% repeat clients and we intend to keep them and all the others aware of the Sierra Motel, even ten years down the line. That means thinking ahead, keeping alive, improving and expanding a bit.

Dick, you've become an expert "moteleer," if that's the word for it. It goes to show what the often reiterated "on-the-job-training" is all about. Providing, of course, that you have the personal resources to maximize it.

It helps to keep the learning process going all the time. Constantly evaluating things, that's part of the process. There's some degree of luck, too, don't forget that. All in all, I guess, things have been working out and Judy and I are both happy about it.

Success-Steps Analysis

Among the personality characteristics necessary for a successful small-business person, "drive" is placed high on the list. Motivation, initiative, and vigor are the components that make up drive.

Dick Oakley doesn't seem lacking in this area. Previously, after his regular work day at the airline, he had built houses for additional income and savings. When it came to purchasing a business, the seven-day work-week requirements of a motel did not dissuade him. And, while they both ran the motel, he additionally immersed himself in contracting and super-vising the restaurant construction. Since then, he is now very involved with both projects (motel and restaurant) and even giving some thought to future planning.

Yet Dick is not a tensed-up, got-to-get-going kind of a guy. He is somewhat relaxed and easy going, perhaps because he uses his time produc-tively and soundly evaluates his priorities, which is important for any kind of successful achievement.

Without a specific enterprise in mind, there was no true preparation in the sense of a business plan, a market study, demographics or production and cost surveys . . .

But there *was* planning . . . and both of the Oakleys participated The finalized decisions for a new life style, their own small business, a well-researched geographic locale, to buy rather than start from scratch, to check out available options and then select . . . all these steps involved planning, not wishful thinking.

The decision for the motel was a result of careful thinking . . . a blend of the initial research with small retailers, a service-career orienta-tion, some previous real-estate experiences, and a good helping of both common and business sense. Dick's building and contracting experience backed up his belief that improvements could be made to the motel. This, in turn, helped with his decision to raise the rate schedule.

The assumable mortgage with the low interest rate, the real-estate appreciation potential, the manageable down payment, the living quarters available, the CPA's involvement, a trusted partner, et cetera, sure there were missing pieces but, all in all, it wasn't a case of closing one's eyes and sending up a flare to attract a guardian angel.

There was the risk element, as there always is.

There was the need for a strong commitment, as there always is.

There was the responsibility of a decision, as there always is.

The Oakleys realized all this—going in. The results during the first year are indicative of how they came to grips with those factors and the many others that crop up in any new business venture. Significantly, Dick Oakley has gone through the initial fires and is no longer apprehensive about the often-required risks and the more-than-modest financial needs. Careful . . . yes. Frightened . . . no!

Many a small-business owner/manager does not have the time or the inclination to get involved with three- and five-year projections or even shorter-ranged structured planning. Their daily involvements and the lack of confidence in their ability to cope with futuristic figures tend to stymie them. In many cases, however, it is being done without the literal analysis and charting that seems so formidable. Planning for future growth or the strong maintenance of your own market share is a must.

Here again, Dick Oakley is filling the bill. Like many in small business, his planning for the future may not be formulated in detail with estimated P & L's, cash flows, marketing strategies, et cetera. But, those partners of "business sense"—perceptiveness and imagination—are definitely there. The apparent need for the restaurant was not just noted and then forgotten. The motel's ability to support a manager was not ignored. His follow-through on acquiring more general motel knowledge and the specific values of motels was not wasted. Most likely the latter helped substantiate the leverage necessary for the restaurant acquisition and some later plans.

Add it all up and it's pretty clear that although Dick Oakley was a novice to the own-your-small-business field, his initial steps and his on-the-job training benefited greatly from his personality characteristics . . . the type of traits that are very meaningful to success-achievement.

Fortunately, he had a good base . . . motivation and drive; initiative and vigor; analytical and creative thinking; the ability to communicate and the often-neglected ability to *use* information . . . i.e., for the very important aspect of the follow-through!

Yes, it takes more than just good personal traits to be successful in small business, but you will almost always find that they are an integral part of the whole. Additionally, some other vital ingredients did enter this picture. There was the team effort of Judy Oakley; a very necessary source of funds from a willing partner; and an exceedingly important bit of luck in that particular motel selection. But keep in mind that all the jigsaw pieces would be meaningless without the opportunity to put them together. And that translates itself into the powerful components of—a willingness to make a commitment and a willingness to take the risk!

It is a truism that small business enables one to be more flexible and to react much more rapidly to opportunity or adversity than a larger business organization allows. It is also true that one must be able to *recognize* these positives and negatives when they first appear, sometimes with professional guidance, often through your own innate feel for things "business."

Update

Recognizing opportunities and the ability to analyze situations seem to be the positives that came out of my second interview with Dick Oakley.

His follow-through on getting a manager for the motel, almost immediately after the first year's operations, was a definite result of ongoing experience and planning. Yes, a judgmental mistake was made, but even that became a learning experience.

Selling the restaurant encompassed a number of entrepreneurial decisions stemming from an economic analysis . . . what to sell, what to retain, the sale price, lease arrangements, and computation of return on investment. It also freed Oakley from supervision time—time he can now devote to the proposed motel expansion.

Commitment is still a definite part of the whole operation, as is the ability to adapt to new situations. Within the first two years, expertise in the chosen field is evident and so is planning ahead. There are many motels in Prescott. Increasing gross sales and profits; buying property across the way for a restaurant; establishing it and selling it profitably; embarking upon a 10-unit expansion . . . these are not the gleanings of simple luck! They are a reflection of the personal resources that Dick Oakley brought with him into the entrepreneurial swim.

The interview with Dick Oakley covered all the areas of how he actually got started in his own small business, but this segment also highlights why I selected him for the chapter heading, "Are You the Type?" Read the interview once again, this time with a greater awareness of his outlook and his personality traits . . . note how they have contributed to his successful start.

Try to evaluate *yourself*—honestly and objectively—to help determine your own personality characteristics as they relate to running your own business.

Ratings of Personal Traits

How important is the question . . . . "Are you the type?"

Any failed or presently successful small-business owner would assure you it's a mandatory preliminary evaluation that must be answered.

Every business counselor, every small-business course, every how-to-start-your-own-business book, would agree that it's the first self-appraisal step to be undertaken.

Of course, there's a lot more to be considered in the process of becoming an entrepreneur. That's exactly the point. Because there are a hundred and one other things you will be concerned with as a small-business owner, it's vital to know if you have the personal resources to cope.

Take the simple, well-established fact that starting your own business means long, long hours, maybe weekends and holidays, too. It's easy to understand the necessity for you to be in good health and to possess all the required energy involved in getting most of the work done yourself.

What about the responsibility of making all the decisions? Handling all the little details? Will you be overwhelmed by this kind of pressure, or can you handle things easily without coming apart?

These and many other questions have to be asked. Spend the time to think about yourself . . . to see if you measure up.

Different businesses often require specific attributes. The owner of a Baskin Robbins franchise stresses the need for a pleasant personality in the retail relationship and a genuine liking for children. Neither of these traits are really necessary for a mail-order operation except, perhaps, in the creative selection of a product.

Another retailer mentioned those depressing times when only one or two shoppers enter the store throughout an entire day. Would you have the stamina for that?

There's a different kind of stamina involved, maybe in a sales or distribution setup, where you're alone in your office and the phone doesn't ring for hours. Is that solitude a problem? Can you handle a series of rejections?

Are you inflexible? Can you change, if the business requires change? Are you willing to take advice from others? Any of these factors may be necessary after consultation with your professional advisors . . . lawyer, accountant, insurance agent and so forth.

Can you absorb new things quickly? Since most beginners are not trained in all the varied managerial aspects . . . the on-the-job learning is crucial.

And there are many more areas to examine. Donald Dible, in his book *Up Your Own Organization,* mentions the three D's . . . Desire, Determination, and Dedication, in addition to Motivation.

All of this examination of the self is to create an awareness about what you need to know about yourself if you wish to go into your own business. If there are too many negatives, don't start. If the self appraisal shows a need to strengthen an area or two, then it has been helpful.

The Small Business Administration booklet, *Starting & Managing a Small Business of Your Own,* notes that "You will be your most important employee. It's more important to rate yourself than it is to rate any prospective employee."

It goes on to mention a number of personality characteristics that were significantly correlated to success. They were drive, thinking ability, human relations ability, communications ability, and technical knowledge.

A rating scale of personal traits, relating mostly to drive, has been reproduced here for an evaluation of your own motivation and drive. Try to be objective and honest. It's better to recognize your weak points before you start. Compensation for them can be made by teaming up with associates or hiring employees whose strong points offset your weak ones.

The booklet also notes that there may be other traits that are necessary for the specific type of business you wish to start. Add those to the list also. Keep in mind that this isn't a scientific, tried and true, authorized test. It's merely a way to make you look yourself over more objectively than you normally would.

Rating Scale for Personal Traits Important to a Business Proprietor

INSTRUCTIONS: After each question place a check mark on the line at the point closest to your answer. The check mark need not be placed directly over one of the suggested answers because your rating may lie somewhere between two answers. Be honest with yourself.

ARE YOU A SELF-STARTER?

| I do things my own way. Nobody needs to tell me to get going. | If someone gets me started, I keep going all right. | Easy does it. I don't put myself out until I have to. |

HOW DO YOU FEEL ABOUT OTHER PEOPLE?

| I like people. I can get along with just about anybody. | I have plenty of friends. I don't need anyone else. | Most people bug me. |

CAN YOU LEAD OTHERS?

| I can get most people to go along without much difficulty. | I can get people to do things if I drive them. | I let someone else get things moving. |

CAN YOU TAKE RESPONSIBILITY?

| I like to take charge of and see things through. | I'll take over if I have to, but I'd rather let someone else be responsible. | There's always some eager beaver around wanting to show off. I say let him. |

HOW GOOD AN ORGANIZER ARE YOU?

| I like to have a plan before I start. I'm usually the one to get things lined up. | I do all right unless things get too goofed up. Then I cop out. | I just take things as they come. |

HOW GOOD A WORKER ARE YOU?

| I can keep going as long as necessary. I don't mind working hard. | I'll work hard for a while, but when I've had enough, that's it! | I can't see that hard work gets you anywhere. |

CAN YOU MAKE DECISIONS?

| I can make up my mind in a hurry if necessary, and my decision is usually o.k. | I can if I have plenty of time. If I have to make up my mind fast, I usually regret it. | I don't like to be the one who decides things. I'd probably blow it. |

CAN PEOPLE TRUST WHAT YOU SAY?

| They sure can. I don't say things I don't mean. | I try to be on the level, but sometimes I just say what's easiest. | What's the sweat if the other fellow doesn't know the difference? |

CAN YOU STICK WITH IT?

| If I make up my mind to do something, I don't let anything stop me. | I usually finish what I start. | If a job doesn't go right, I turn off. Why beat your brains out? |

HOW GOOD IS YOUR HEALTH?

| I never run down. | I have enough energy for most things I want to do. | I run out of juice sooner than most of my friends seem to. |

Source: SBA's Starting & Managing Series, Vol. 1, 3rd edition "Starting & Managing a Small Business of Your Own"

2 Testing the Market

Richard Iozzo is a builder.

He builds houses to order . . . all styles.

He and his wife, Ann Marie, maintain a showroom in a suburban village.

There are many model homes on display there, and one can purchase anything in furnishings for the house . . . kitchen equipment, furniture, brass beds, chandeliers.

Their only restriction is . . . everything is no bigger than dollhouse size!

ANGELA'S DOLL HOUSE *
PELHAM, NEW YORK

There are many ways in which a small business gets started. Sometimes it happens almost by chance . . . more often after a good deal of soul-searching and brain-burning.

Richard Iozzo and his wife were fortunate to have combined both when they officially opened their venture in a Westchester suburb of New York City.

Richard, at that time in his early thirties, had always been involved with cabinet-making projects in his after-work hours. His extensively-equipped workshop in the basement of their home was the result of an accumulation that started during his teen-age years.

Dollhouses and miniatures . . . offhand, it doesn't seem to be a business with a future. Is there opportunity for growth?

For all I know this could be a fad, but I don't think so. The amount of research I've done and the contacts I now have throughout the country tell me that the business is going to reach a level, probably in the next five years, of ten to twenty times the present volume and then, most likely, level off and stay there. By that time there will be a tremendous number of people relating to the field. And there's always replacement involved. A dollhouse is just like a regular house, there's plenty of activity going on . . . remodeling, repairing, trading up, and so on. It's the exact same thing . . . it's the real world in miniature! Right now, in my custom-order services, I'm working on houses . . . adding wings, renovating, rewiring, redecorating, adding new additions . . .

How did you get into all this? I see lots of inventory and equipment around, and neither you nor Ann Marie were into this kind of hobby before.

I've always been interested in architectural design . . . always enjoyed working with my hands. I'm the type of person who likes to take a project from beginning to end. When I was a production manager for a manufacturing firm, my job was taking something from inception to delivery, getting involved with the coordination of engineering, production, manufacturing and selling. And all the time I was working, even during the ten years of nights at the community college, I kept doing cabinet work on the side, handling various projects and building up my workshop. I guess that's how the whole dollhouse thing got started.

There was a craft shop in the vicinity and the woman who ran it knew of my cabinet work. She told me that a number of customers were interested in buying dollhouses for their children, but didn't want to pay the going price for them . . . $150 to $200. She asked if I would be interested in making a few that she would sell on a consignment basis. Well, I figured, "why not" and I later asked a modest $40 price for each. And, although she usually marks things up from one-third to 100%, this time she decided to add only ten dollars to my figure. Guess she didn't really believe in the market, even though it was her idea.

I made my own very basic house design and finished five simple dollhouses for her . . . it was just before the holiday season. Sure enough, they all sold very quickly.

Was that the incentive to start out on your own?

No, not exactly. It was still something new. But, I thought then, maybe I had an item that could earn me some extra money. So I placed an ad in the local papers and offered to build dollhouses, asking $50 for an unfinished house and $75 for a house with a painted exterior and some other finishing touches. It was great . . . the response was for fifteen houses.

Building them wasn't the problem, not with my workshop . . . it was the time. I usually worked on the dollhouse before my regular job at the phone company, where I work a four p.m. to midnight shift. Because I did everything myself . . . doors, windows, and all that . . . each house took weeks and weeks to finish.

> *No percentage there. Not enough profit per unit and not enough time to handle more units.*

Exactly. And that's when Ann Marie started to send for more information about the field . . . catalogs, trade magazines, anything that could help. It was a real eye-opener for the both of us. The items that were available were mind-boggling. I had no idea that practically everything you needed for building dollhouses was available . . . dormers, windows, mouldings, electrical fixtures, wiring, doors, staircases . . . the whole works. It was absolutely fascinating.

Anne Marie: That's when we decided to look into the commercial world of dollhouses and miniatures. We were both hooked on the idea of trying to make a go with our own business, especially if we could get into it gradually . . . like Richard had been doing. And, by the way, that's how it went. We didn't just pop into this business. It took almost a year of study and research, a lot of common sense, and some good advice from a few of our suppliers before we opened the doors.

> *Richard, I guess your previous production experience and college business courses helped, too.*

Yes and no. It's not like the planning I did in manufacturing. There you get tied up with lots of forms and paperwork. When you get into small business, you really have to wing it a bit, initially . . . things are changing so fast. We *did* have a plan of attack . . . didn't always follow it, naturally. But after this long period of research, we did sit down and map out the details: What we wanted to get into . . . what the basis of our business should be . . . what inventory should be stocked and the starting costs, approximately. We decided to have a small shop that was convenient to our home, because that's where all the woodworking equipment was. I would continue my regular job and use the off-hours to design and build houses and remodel them. Ann Marie would be running the shop and selecting the inventory. She's quite creative with her hands and her mind, and has a good knack for sensing what people really go for. She has taught both primary and secondary classes and likes teaching very much, but is somewhat disenchanted with today's education.

Ann Marie is not the type who is happy sitting at home. Our second child was born not long before we opened the shop, so running the business provided her with a good opportunity to keep working. The shop was named after our baby daughter, Angela. Fortunately, we have a large family and relatives nearby and they have been wonderful in helping to care for the children. Our son, who's now ten, was also a part of that kind of extended family care when Ann Marie went back to teaching a year after he was born.

How did you select a location and handle start-up capital for initial inventory and starting expenses?

Location was important in more ways than one. It had to be close to our home in Mt. Vernon, where all the major equipment is located. Convenience to both workshops is mandatory when you may need something from one or the other to complete a project. For customers, Pelham is extremely convenient . . . it's near the parkways and there is sufficient parking in town. The reasonable rent was a big factor . . . and since our business is a specialty one, our customers are willing to travel and seek us out. Therefore, a high-traffic shopping area is *not* a must for us.

We also checked to verify that there is really nothing in the surrounding area quite like our operation. Hobby shops carry some things we do and toy stores carry some similar things, but there wasn't any true competition.

When it came to start-up capital, we retained our original idea of taking it slow, one step at a time. We knew the inventory we wanted to start out with; our rent was low; there were no salaries to pay; so the initial budgeting was very modest.

I've always had a good rapport with one bank on a personal basis. Luckily the banker that I was dealing with has a hobby of model railroading . . . so he could identify with me and with our ideas. We weren't asking for that large an amount of money, either . . . $5,000. The loan was being taken out on a personal basis rather than on a business basis.

That seems to be pretty low "starting-out" money. Was it enough?

It was, at the time. Don't forget, there were no salaries and Ann Marie and I were the only ones working. It was enough to take care of the initial inventory, the rent and utilities, and the setting up of a corporation. Later on, I also put up another $5,000, so that first year required $10,000.

Another important factor was my existing workshop. If you had to go out and buy all that equipment, setting up a business like ours would cost from $25,000 to $35,000.

By the way, we now have a $5,000 credit line. Not big . . . but enough for cash flow when we need it. In other words, after two years the books have shown up well enough for the bank to believe in us. You have to have some kind of a business history, you can't do it the first year. Sometimes not even the second.

And, as a base, you always have the income from your jobs to sustain you along the way.

Right. Being an employee gives you a very necessary sense of security. You cannot enter or develop a business like this and just burn your bridges behind you, believe me. The last thing in the world you want to do is give up a full-time job . . . which I still haven't done. It makes doing this a lot easier when you can sleep at night knowing that you're going to be able to provide for your family and have food on the table.

And let's face it, you really don't know whether a business is going to work or not. You're talking something like five years minimum, and if you can make it through that five-year period and show a profit, you can be pretty sure that you're going to be in business a while longer. Of course, if you get rapped with a recession, like we did a number of years ago, that's another story. Many small business went right down the drain, even though they had been in business for a few years or more.

Ann Marie: We opened in the fall and that gave us a chance to take advantage of the Christmas season . . . that's when the majority of our sales occur. But that first year was full of uncertainties. It was our baptism into the small-business arena. I don't know how, but we did manage a profit that first year. The next Christmas season was even better . . . 100% better!

No salaries have been taken, thus far, and all the profits have been reinvested. This is not a business you just jump into. We feel we're developing a unique line of products and that we will succeed in the future.

Richard: It's more advantageous for us, as long as we can work it that way, to build and strengthen the business. A lot of people who go into business say, "Aha, I'm going to make a killing, take it off the top and live." But you *can't go* into business that way. Your creditors creep up on your back door pretty quickly. You know . . . thirty days go by awfully fast!

You mentioned incorporating a while back. Why did you select that form of business?

We would not open the doors without setting up a corporation. The reason has nothing to do with creditors or bankruptcies. It was done for peace of mind. Children are involved in this type of business . . . coming in with their parents. Should some accident happen, I want that barrier between my business and my personal life. I don't want to sacrifice my home or life for something that I may not even be responsible for.

Sure, I carry liability insurance . . . you have to! You would be stupid if you didn't. A corporation is a little more expensive and there's a lot more paperwork . . . it can be a pain, at times . . . but it's insurance. My attorney tried to talk me out of it, but I said no, I want to feel comfortable when I walk into the shop.

Also, Ann Marie and I are *equal* partners in the stock of the corporation. She's very cognizant, especially since she started in business, of the fact that you have to protect that business investment. We're at the point where if something happened to one or both of us . . . we don't want the business to die. We've made provisions . . . there are a lot of things that people who start a business just don't realize.

*What about the books . . . there is more paperwork
with a corporate setup. Did you have an accountant when
you started?*

As a matter of fact, we did not start with an accountant. I had some
background in business . . . marketing, specifically. I hated accounting!
It was one of those initial decisions where money was tight. An accountant
doesn't do his thing for nothing . . . and I just didn't feel like commiting
the dollars. I knew what was coming in and what was going out and I had a
checkbook. Along with that, we set up a rudimentary bookkeeping system
and both of us maintained it.

Later, when we could manage, the accountant came in and took over those
first six or eight months of paperwork. He used total figures and started out
fresh from there. He set up a better system and comes in regularly to do
what he has to do.

Ann Marie took care of the bookkeeping, originally. Now I do. Generally
on a Saturday when I'm in, I'll sit down with the books, do the bills, the
receivables, and so on. After all, she still has a family to raise and a home to
run . . . and that takes plenty of time, too. In fact, now that we are
starting our third year, we are hiring our first full-time employee . . . a
young relative.

*Richard, those first steps in running a business can be
either a disaster or a triumph. What were some of the
misses and hits at Angela's?*

Well, you mentioned "learning on the job" and there's a lot of truth there.
At the beginning we felt that we should have something for everyone who
came into the shop. If a mother came in with her daughter and her son, we
should have some wooden toys for the son. We've since wiped that out.
Initially it seemed to make sense, but you're taking away from the main
thrust of your business. I used to do cabinet work, so I had one section of the
original store set up with displays of the things we did . . . wood turnings,
small shelves. Again, not only taking space away, but also taking the thrust
away from our main business.

We finally decided to devote the whole business to a specific type of
situation. In our case, it's dollhouse construction. There are other shops

that deal strictly in miniatures, which gets more into the furnishings end. Of course, we also have furnishings. We'd be foolish not to. You have to have some ancillary products for the person that comes in and buys a house for a child for Christmas and then wants to furnish a room. We have found that you've got to learn your clientele and it's going to take a year, two, or three years. We are now getting in some finer pieces, collector pieces, that we feel we have a market for. But what has allowed us to do that is the fact that we haven't really been greedy about the business, we've been turning the money back into the business and expanding that way.

Then there was the mail-order catalog and the wholesaling to others. These ideas were in our original planning, but came sooner than we had anticipated.

This is the type of business that is definitely seasonal. There's a somewhat affluent society here and in the summer there are golf, boating, vacations, summer homes, and so on. You can't rely on retail trade, so you have to provide a supplementary income. That's why the catalog was something we *had* to do, and it had to be done quickly. We almost didn't do it . . . but you've got to take some chances. During our first year there were a lot of sleepless nights in the summertime. People find it hard to believe that a shopkeeper might only do $5 worth of business in one day. It happens, especially in a new business.

The catalog has been a major step for us, because it gives us a national market and keeps us from being dependent . . . totally dependent on the walk-in or holiday trade. We couldn't keep going without it. We advertise in our trade journals and are now trying some of the craft magazines. Probably we don't do as much advertising as we should . . . we do as much as we can afford. Angela's catalog sells for $2.50 and it's already paid for itself. We also send out information flyers at no charge, if you send a stamped, addressed envelope.

In general, then, you've shaken out the kinks and the prognosis looks pretty healthy?

I think so. We've now completed our second year in business. This present store is the third move we've made on this block . . . due to growth and space requirements. Now there's plenty of floor space for a dozen or more display houses and we stock more styles of doors, windows, staircases, dormers, and mouldings than you can find in a regular lumber yard. My basic house design—a Williamsburg-like colonial—is copyrighted and a round window I developed, which can fit into any dollhouse, has been patented. We've packaged houseplans of my designs for both retail and wholesale sales. The custom-made houses keep me busy and I don't have time anymore for cabinet work. Just like building a real house, some of my customers will meet with me for months at a time until we have all the design ideas worked out.

You have to understand that these houses aren't toys. Many are masterpieces in miniature and they're for adults . . . just like any hobby. The adults are really the ones who get totally involved in details and quality. We're geared primarily to the middle-of-the-road buyer. You can get into this hobby on all levels . . . from the inexpensive to thousands of dollars for a single piece of furniture. We have avoided the inexpensive items because of the lack of quality that exists there.

I have built houses for their therapeutic value. A doctor whose daughter had a learning disability reported a great improvement in her condition . . . we had designed a house especially for her. Others tell me they go home at night, get occupied with additional work on their houses and find no need to drink, or smoke, or be bored . . . just a great way to unwind.

Ann Marie, what about the catalogs and your newsletter? How are they working out?

The catalogs are Richard's developments. His marketing background was a great help when we had to get moving so quickly. There were fifty pages in that first one and most of it had to be professionally done . . . layouts, photos, typeset, and so on. Luckily he had a good rapport with a printer who really gave us sound advice.

For next year, we are putting out a sixteen page supplement to the catalog and on this one Richard has done practically everything . . . especially the layouts, which can be so costly. Our mailing list has gone over the 1,000 mark and my newsletter goes to all on that list twice a year.

The four-page newsletter includes what's new at Angela's, hints and suggestions from customers, publications in the field, a calendar of shows, and often a short piece on a particularly interesting period and style of furnishings. I really enjoy putting it out.

Richard: And, it's good, too! All of this "doing-it-ourselves" from the very beginning has helped tremendously to keep us in line with our original thought of trying out a small business . . . seeing if it will work. It's a lot of commitment for both of us! Ann Marie with a family and a home, but here at the store all day and I with my regular job, but putting all my spare time into the business.

Like the catalog . . . you can't just hire everybody to do things for you. Sometimes you have to, but if you feel you can get away with doing your own layouts, then do it. Or if you can do your own photography, do it. In advertising, if you can, deal with publications that will do all the layouts for you and pick up the production charges.

Incidentally, I had to put in the extra $5,000 because we hadn't figured on the expense of a catalog in our small initial start-up capital. Fortunately, it's been paid back.

Although we could do more advertising if we had more dollars, we have had a lot of help in another direction. There've been a number of feature stories and articles on Angela's Doll House in the local newspapers and trade magazines. My marketing experience gave me some pointers there . . . write something, then always follow up with a call or visit.

What about your regular job? Will you go into this full time . . . is this what you had in mind all along?

My present job is o.k. But my company is in the same position as many large companies in relation to affirmative-action programs and chances for advancement. I'm in the type of job that pays me a fairly decent salary . . . it's convenient . . . but I wanted more than that. And, if I can't go ahead with them and advance a few steps, well, I'll have to do it on my own.

One thing is for sure: Whatever happens, this has been and *is* a great experience. I thoroughly enjoy having full control and exercising the decisions that go with it. To accomplish things on your own is terrific, and we both get a great satisfaction and sense of confidence in ourselves from that. It's been a challenge and we're meeting it . . . so far, successfully!

Success-Steps Analysis

Many a beginning entrepreneur, although loaded with enthusiasm, often approaches his or her own business with a somewhat less than confident outlook. Perhaps that isn't all bad. If they had a chance, of course, they would dearly love to try it out first . . . dip a toe into the boiling water, so to speak, to see if they can stand the boil; if their product or service is right. But it's pretty difficult in most cases to literally *audition* a prospective small business.

With Richard and Ann Marie, however, there was a way . . . one that started by chance, yes . . . but one that was further developed by planning and clear thinking. Specific procedures that can easily be reviewed and copied by those readers who wish to enter the small business arena . . . slowly!

The basis of Richard Iozzo's consignment sales of five houses was his craft skills and a well-stocked woodworking shop . . . both resulting from a long-time hobby. These were existing assets that were completely applicable to a small business in an allied area. Starting with that kind of base is one sure way of lessening the risk of entering the small-business arena.

He experimented with a small ad to test the marketplace and check out both the acceptability and the need for a product he was now familiar with. The fifteen response-sales to his ad were actual orders, which negated the usual necessity of an initial speculation. It also encouraged him to think about starting a business in this market.

Going into business was no snap decision for the Iozzos. Research went on for more than a year in an effort to get complete information about the field. Then they decided what they wanted to do. In effect they followed the initial steps often advocated . . . study your industry, your product, your market; get guidance from the trade publications and your suppliers; then make a plan. Their business plan was not the structured one that every beginner tends to shy away from. It was, instead, a fairly simple but thorough statement of "what are we doing?" and "how are we going to do it?" And their answers to those questions would naturally include . . . the type of business, its emphasis, the location, competition, approximate costs, and who was going to do what. Those really are the basics of any plan; best of all, the questions were asked before any business was started.

When they started, Richard did not give up his regular job. He treated the new business as a secondary source of income; its potential was to be determined later. By his decision to continue using his own designs, he enhanced an established product with a specific identity and marketing difference.

The addition of Ann Marie as an integral and active partner was both sound and extremely helpful. A small business requires a firm commitment of one's energies and time, often to the detriment of a marriage and family life. Working together can create mutual goals and enthusiasm, in addition to providing the initial oft-required inexpensive helping hand. Her part-ship, in this case, was vital if Richard was to retain his job and the initial capital requirements remain low.

Throughout the first two years, no salaries were paid and all profits were put back into the business. It meant lots of time and effort on both their parts but it was also the most productive way to build from scratch with the base support of a steady income from another source.

Their very modest start-up loan of $5,000 was a personal one. Initial capital is difficult, almost impossible to get from any bank, so most beginners have to use their own resources. The Iozzos did find a "kindred soul" banker, however, and it's always been suggested that you *shop* for a bank or a loan, until you get the best terms and assistance for your venture. Today Angela's Doll House, with a modest track record as a business, has established a beginning bank credit line of $5,000, which Richard said is mandatory to keep up with a practical cash flow in certain seasonal adjust-ments.

Your market, in any business, must be large enough to support the growth and profitability of your venture. If it isn't, you must search out a way to increase that market, or be forced to close down. The mail-order catalog was a sound move in this direction, as was the wholesale aspect . . . both moves were additive ones that opened their market considerably. They were started when needed! These factors and the one establishing Richard's own designs were risks, of course, but the risk principle shows up in every entrepreneurial endeavor . . . especially the successful ones.

Admittedly, their capitalization was weak in the start-up stage. But with no salaries to pay, a well-established skill that relates to the business, a fully-equipped workshop already paid for, and a steady income from a regular job . . . this was not as catastrophic as it might have been. It was also the right combination to get them started in a small business without prior experience and without excessive risk. Still, a second infusion of capital was required to develop another outlet for sales and sales develop-ment. Double check *your* capital requirements; if correctly estimated, this can help ensure success in starting a small business.

So far, so good. But keep in mind that it will still require lots of effort from the Iozzos to keep their business going and growing. Their commitment is obvious and, hopefully, the returns on their efforts will be further realized in the near future. Of great importance to each of them was their gradual step-by-step approach . . . pledging their total efforts and skills . . . meeting each challenge in turn and succeeding from an almost zero-base to an established entrepreneurship.

Here again, this interview covered all aspects of the Iozzo's emergence as developers and managers of their own small business. And, all the interviews follow the same mode. But each in turn will also offer a clearer insight into a specific fundamental aspect of small business.

Richard and Ann Marie have shown us a series of steps that worked for them, that enabled them to *test* the business marketplace gradually and with a reduced risk factor.

Starting Part-Time

Without doubt, starting a small business is one of the riskiest undertakings around. Banks avoid granting loans for this purpose because they are not in the gambling business. The failure-rate statistics for new businesses certainly bear this out.

But for anyone who entertains the thought of becoming a small entrepreneur, that's only part of the story. They are also plagued with apprehension as to their own abilities and knowledge, their reception in the marketplace, and the many other unknown factors that govern their potential for success.

If it's their first time "going it alone," how can they be sure of handling it all? Must they be "expert" before they start? Can everything, or at least the most important managerial factors, be learned on the job? Are they picking the right product, service, skill? Or will they add to the failure statistics?

Sometimes it's best to learn the business by taking a full or part-time job in the field you have selected for your specific venture. In this way you may gain a working knowledge of how that business is conducted, the pricing factors, suppliers, advertising approach, market area, range of consumers, et cetera.

As in the case of the Iozzos, the answer may lie in the principle of testing . . . testing both the marketplace and your own desires and determination. By starting out slowly, via a part-time endeavor that relates to your special skills, hobby, or specific interests, you can acquire the least costly learning experience.

Keeping your present job and exploring the potential for starting a small business in your spare time offers both security and the opportunity for a modest risk. This type of effort provides on-the-job training and a good test of your product or service in the marketplace. You also become familiar with the entrepreneurial mandatories of record-keeping, pricing, regulation of cash flow, advertising and promotion, competitor evaluation, and profitability.

The additional benefits inherent in following the part-time path to ownership are many:

> no large capital investment required
> the potential to operate from a home base
> the potential for a family venture
> the opportunity to earn as you learn
> the exploitation of existing skills or hobbies
> time to verify the business potential
> expansion, as needed, into a full-time business

The types of businesses that can function successfully within a part-time structure are almost limitless. Whether they involve skills, manufacture, service, or mail-order, the varieties within each category run into the hundreds. And there's plenty of helpful information available in your public library, local bookstores, or through government agencies.

It's imperative to do some reading, in order to stimulate your own thoughts and to absorb some of the how-to aspects of business. In reviewing just a handful of the many books available, I was impressed by the part-time possibilities that existed in:

> the mail order of services instead of products
> the variety of services to homes and individuals
> the variety of services to industry and institutions
> the modest franchises for spare-time operations
> the variety of applications for existing skills
> the home manufacture of specialty products
> your kitchen as a possible money-making source

Admittedly, many of the ideas offered by these books are not sure-fire! But at the same time there may be opportunities mentioned that you may not have thought about. And that's part of the reason for reading . . . to start you thinking and perhaps looking for additional information. Then, maybe, the process of evaluation comes into play, and before you know it, an idea gells.

Some books surface-explore related areas that are meaningful to small-business ownership. A few books will indicate where additional information can be obtained. Generating enthusiasm, however, is one of their main functions . . . perhaps their primary one. So for detailed information on the nitty-gritties and pitfalls of starting and operating a small business, you will have to add a few other more comprehensive volumes to the bookshelf.

If you do start with a part-time operation, make sure you continue to follow-up and study the field you've selected. Prepare yourself for future expansion and the inevitable managerial responsibilities that accompany growth. Although you will usually start out as a sole proprietor, consider that at a later time you may wish to organize your business as a partnership or corporation.

Helpful Reading

Parker Publishing (a division of Prentice-Hall, Inc.) puts out a great deal of material in the "get-rich-quick-and-easy" school. The books are definitely meant to enthuse and inspire the potential entrepreneur. Many are concerned with the part-time venture and contain very useful information.

Second Income Money Makers (1975), by Scott Witt

How to Make Big Profits in Service Businesses (1977), by Scott Witt

The Complete Handbook of How to Start and Run a Money-Making Business in Your Home (1975), by Marian Behan Hammer

How to Start Your Own Business On a Shoestring and Make up to $100,000 a Year (1968), by Tyler G. Hicks

100 Ways to Make Money in Your Spare Time, Starting With Less Than $100 (1972), by John Stockwell and Herbert Holtie

Other publishers . . .

How to Start and Operate a Mail-Order Business (1976), by Julian L. Simon. McGraw-Hill.

How To Profit From Arts and Crafts (1978), by Albert and Carol Lee. David McKay.

1001 Ways to Be Your Own Boss (1976), by Vivo Bennett and Cricket Clagett. Prentice-Hall.

How to Make Money in Your Kitchen (1977), by Jeffrey Feinman. William Morrow.

100 Sure-Fire Businesses You Can Start With Little or No Investment (1976), by Jerry Feinman. Playboy Press.

Treasury of Business Opportunities . . . Featuring Over 400 Ways to Make a Fortune Without Leaving Your Home (1976), by David D. Soltz. Farnsworth.

How to Make Money in the Flea Market (1978), by Joan Bursten and Louanne Norris. Dutton.

Mail Order . . . Starting Up, Making it Pay (1979), by J. Frank Brumbaugh. Chilton.

How to Start and Run a Profitable Craft Business (1977), Archie Ossin and Myrna Ossin. Wiley.

How to Sell Your Artwork: A Complete Guide for Fine and Commercial Artists (1978), by Milton K. Berlye, Prentice-Hall.

3   A Business Plan

Ken Dean set out for a city he had never been to before . . . to involve himself in something he had never done before.

He knows more about business management than any other person in this book, but that didn't make going into a small business of his own any less formidable.

Admittedly, what he did know enabled him to follow the often risky pattern of buying an existing business and paying for it out of the profits that the business would—hopefully—generate.

AIR FILTER SERVICE *
TUCSON, ARIZONA

In searching for a distributor or manufacturer to interview in Tucson, a business broker suggested that I try to interest Ken Dean, who "is a real pro."

When I did, it only took a minute or two to confirm the broker's appraisal. Ken took off with very little prodding and my questions were answered almost before they were asked. So, here goes . . . not too many questions, but plenty of thoughtful answers.

Ken, just give us some background . . . your previous jobs, philosophies, how you became an entrepreneur, and so on . . .

I'm 44 years old. I spent the last 10 years of my life working in various senior capacities with big companies. I specialized in having companies that had divisions that were in the red come to me and I was able to turn them around, usually in 90 days, to the start of something better. After a period of fine-tuning with one company, someone else would call me in to another job and another corporation.

I'm a generalist. My major in college was business and philosophy. I felt early on that I should know something about the many facets of business, so I started out in sales and then got into the operational aspects, because that was where you could really make money for the corporation. I started doing some financing work and that type of thing.

When I was going from corporation to corporation, I would go in, make a survey of what their problems were from the viewpoint of operations, marketing, administration, or whatever, and then give them a plan. If we agreed on the plan, then I would implement it. My only condition was that they make me the general manager or the vice president in charge, with full overall responsibility.

If I didn't meet the goals set in my plan, they could fire me on a moment's notice. I wanted a salary, no bonuses, and we took it from there. In every instance, as I say, we turned around usually in 90 days. Very seldom did we have to change personnel. It's just that big corporations have no idea how to put things together. They aren't doers. The one thing I didn't have to worry about at all was money. The big corporations were so used to losing money that when all of a sudden I'd start changing that and cut their losses by 30% within the first month or two, they thought I was super.

Where did you handle most of this activity? Did Tucson figure into it and is that why you're here?

Literally all over. Since 1970 I've averaged 100,000 miles in airplanes.

No, six months ago I didn't know where Tucson was. I came back from Europe in November. My wife and I were having dinner one night and I had a $75,000-a-year job and I was getting ready to be promoted to the senior position in the corporation, and I said, "You know, you'll think I'm crazy but I'm going to quit all this bull!" I said I was going to go to Tucson because I had never been there before and I was going to look for a business, any kind of business.

My rationale was this: I had $60,000 cash . . . seven years ago I didn't have a penny; I was flat broke and owed a lot of money. I had $60,000 cash and I had desire. I figured I was still young enough so that if I failed, I would still be able to come back to the major corporations.

Sounds like you might have had a dream. Did she agree?

Oh, no. Not at all. Not then. But coincidentally . . . next week she's finally coming down. She's sold the house in Stamford and she's coming down for better or for worse. This will be a definite change.

But, getting back . . . I got to Tucson about the last week in November and was going to spend three weeks looking for businesses here. My rationale for the southwest was that, number one, it's a growing area. Florida is growing also, but I don't like Florida. I was going to try Phoenix, which is an ideal place. But I thought if Phoenix is good, Tucson might be a little bit more provincial, and offer a little more in the way of opportunities. If it wasn't here in Tucson, then I was going to go back to the original idea of Phoenix. If I didn't find anything in Phoenix, I was going to San Diego and from San Diego I was going to go to Las Vegas. Those were the key areas. I had no particular business in mind. In the last 20 years I've been part of a fully-integrated steel mill, I've had 52 service stations, I ran a shower-door business, I've been in paperboard packaging . . . so I had a rounded background.

I looked in the paper and I didn't really concentrate on any one type of business. All I was looking for was the right vehicle. I looked at a doughnut shop, for instance. I looked at buying three 7-11 stores; I looked at anything that would give me the return based on some sound management. Again, I'm a generalist.

The business I bought was a failing business. It had been here for 26 years, father and son, and the son took it over. He increased sales but eventually dissipated things. Based on their books, no one wanted to buy. For four years they had lost six or seven thousand a year at least, out of about $240,000 in sales. I looked at the books and took out all of the baloney I could find there and said . . . well, this is what I think it would cost me to run the business, and I wrote a program. I'm a great one for programs, so that I have a guide as to where I'm going.

They had $240,000 in sales and I said if anything can't grow 15% a year it's not worth it. So I made a projection based on $280,000 worth of business a year. I took out what I thought my expenses were going to be and I decided what my risk was worth in terms of a return to me. I can get eight percent on my money anyplace, so I figured for another six percent . . . that's the risk factor. I had to get a fourteen percent return on *net* sales, not on my investment. I worked all the numbers back and forth and it turned out that it was 13.9. I didn't force anything, I just let the figures fall where they were.

> *O.K., because of your strong business background, the "any vehicle with the correct return" principle made a lot of sense. For the usual beginner, that kind of approach might be difficult. What did this business actually consist of and what were the financial details?*

They started out here by manufacturing air filters for refrigeration and heating for both homes and businesses. I said to hell with the manufacturing end of it, it was archaic. I didn't buy it and now it's a dead issue. Initially they wanted $120,000 for the total business. We settled on $65,000 without the manufacturing, of which $20,000 was good will. I never argued the good will part because in the back of my mind I figured by the time I got around to paying that on the terms I was going to get, they would be 25-cent dollars. I got them to finance the purchase price . . . again this was a dying business. I got them to finance it for 15 years at seven percent. They had two choices when they sold this business . . . they could go bankrupt in a short while, if it was their choice, or we could take over and at least they would be getting $65,000 over a specific period.

> *That's a pattern that usually works when negotiating for a failing business or an overpriced one. Especially if there are no other offers around. When you closed the deal, you gave no cash up front?*

That's right. Not a penny. I was also ready to walk away from it if they didn't want to accept my terms. I did put $20,000 down, but that $20,000 all went into inventory. When I got here, they had $6,000 worth of inventory and we now have about $60,000, which we own every penny of.

I've been fortunate that when I came here they had—well, let's see, there are four manufacturers of our filter products in the United States of any consequence. Two of them really don't sell west of the Mississippi. Of the other two, one of them is the biggest in the world and the other is a very strong regional one. We already represented the strong regional one.

I then went to the national manufacturer, who is the biggest one in the industry, and convinced them that since they weren't doing any business here anyway, we could represent the state for them, even though, you know, it would have to be a dual thing. I talked both companies into letting me do that (representing both the national and regional ones). Since that time we've taken all the business in the state, all the business in the counties, and all the business in the cities.

We've been in business five months now and on the $280,000 projection we have already $125,000 in sales after the fifth month and we are netting, after tax, about eighteen percent on net sales. This includes my salary—I pay myself $1,200, a month, and that's quite a comedown from $5,000 or $6,000 a month. We've borrowed money from the bank not because we wanted to but simply because we wanted to show them we have the ability to pay it off. I don't have the purchase order but I've just been told that I've closed a deal for $250,000, that will fall due before the 15th of September of this year. So, fortunately, we're quite a bit ahead of schedule.

For me the biggest shock was the second day I was here, unloading my own trucks. I'm used to having a foreman doing that kind of stuff, but when you're not contributing anyplace else or feeling you're not, there's something about physical activity that makes you think . . . God, at least I'm doing something.

And you take the people—everything I've ever done, it isn't me. It's really the ability I've had to work with people, to find people . . . a lot of luck . . . you generate a spirit, if you will, by your own enthusiasm.

I have people come to me and say, "Hey, I want to get in to whatever you're going to get into." I have a partner here, a junior partner who was working with me when I built a few plants; he's a good example. Two years ago he was making $10,000 a year . . . when he finished working for me, he was making $35,000. He gave that up to come to work here, the same as me. People may think we're crazy, but we know what we're doing. Again, it's the risk. Someone who is willing to take the risk. And there's a certain satisfaction at the end of the month, you know. That's our report card.

But, admittedly, it's a calculated risk . . . a knowledge-
able one. Not someone going ahead, hoping it will work.
You had a thorough business plan . . . based on experi-
ence and facts, not wishful thinking.

Yes, but the plan is just a guide. At the same time I'm not emotionally involved. Just in the short time I've been here . . . someone has offered to buy this business and I could probably make about $35,000 out of it. It's crazy because the guy is all emotional and you have to take the emotionalism out of it. I told Paul, my partner, who has twenty percent of the business here . . . I said if you get a job offer for $50,000 take it, don't have any qualms, because if I get one for $75,000 to $100,000, I may take it. I have a certain criterion and if this business falls below a certain return for two months in a row, I'm going to sell the business. That's the only way I know how to operate.

Did you take Paul in as a partner after you had made the
decision and put up your initial investment?

No. He's a friend and I asked him to come down because I didn't want to be emotional about my own judgment here. You know, there was a lot involved, throwing all my money in, my wife not too happy. I had him review the deal, and while he doesn't have all the business background, he has the facility of asking me questions that I might not ask myself.

As we finished and as he was getting on the plane . . . we did this in about 12 hours . . . he said, "I'll send you a check for $10,000. You can count on me for that." I hadn't asked him for any money, but this is the kind of relationship that we have.

We have a clear understanding of who runs the company. I can show you the profiles and descriptions of everyone's responsibilities in this company for the next three years. I believe that once you give the responsibility and everyone understands it, there are no more questions about it, you've got your business. I formed a corporation, Quixote Enterprises, Inc. The main idea was to be successful enough so that at the end of three years we could either sell it to someone, or go public, or be in that position. I really don't have any desire to become a limiting factor. We have four people working here, including Paul and myself. Previously almost 12 people worked here.

Our other two people, the office secretary and sales engineer, they can see the profit-sharing, based on their own efforts, and they can see every month when we read the books. There are no secrets. I don't make any mysteries out of the damn thing.

Ken, prior to and including your corporate life, had you ever been your own entrepreneur? And if not, why now?

Never! I've had a lot of desire but no courage. Corporation coward, I think. The only difference I find is I can better control the money, and I don't have to answer to anyone. I've always managed other people's money, but that's all; now I watch the cash flow, I keep the leverage. Besides I don't like wearing three-piece suits anymore.

Before the interview, we were discussing some of the basic aspects of business, things that many of our management theorists and bankers don't relate to.

As I said earlier, none of them have ever had to sweat out a payroll, *personally* sweat it out. That's what really separates the men from the boys. Every successful entrepreneur that I've known personally knows what it's like to go out and crawl over every junk yard for the parts he needs because he can't go down to the store and pick them up.

People in corporations today . . . the sharp young men in middle management . . . they have no sense of reality. That distortion of reality ruins you in building a business simply because there's a corporate sugar daddy, who in some mystic way . . . even though you know you're losing money, or you're not making your nut . . . will keep those checks coming to you. I think that's why most people should stay with corporations, frankly. Management to me, or the definition of management to me, is someone who will take risks. There are hardly any risk-takers these days in corporations. So my approach with corporations was a maverick one. I got results simply because I was willing to take some risks. Not *crazy* risks, but risks.

The biggest complaint that I have against corporations and why I finally took some risks when I got into one, is that I got tired of being the individual who . . . Let's say there are ten steps in creating something. They'd come along to me and say, "Hey Ken, step No. 6 is yours." You weren't to question where it came from, and more importantly, where it was going. I'm not built that way and a lot of my peers are not built that way, but they learned to accept the system. And those of us that wanted to know why, we got into a lot of people's hair. But at least we developed some insights from that. I don't have all the answers, that's for damned sure, but at least I know where to go when I spot a problem—you know, if I'm sick, I call a doctor, and if I have a legal problem, I'll go to a lawyer. You do pretty much the same thing in business.

That's a good point to pursue. How did you relate to professional help in evaluating the deal?

I didn't know anyone in town. But I've been lucky. In the first week I met some influential people . . . literally on the street. When I worked out my plan, I went to Jack Davis, president of the Southern Division of United Bank. He looked at the program and thought I was crazy, but he said, "I like your style." I wasn't asking for money then. I said I wanted a bank that I can grow with if I do things.

I spent a lot of money up front and most people may not. I went to Lovett and Horwacker, one of the big five international accounting firms. They've got an office here and I gave them my own plan to review *before* I closed the deal. I paid them $800 and they tore everything apart and I think out of a projected budget of $280,000, they were $2,000 off from what I came up with, in my favor. Then they helped me set up the books, they got everything going for me so that I could say, hey I started the business the right way. I had all the benefit of someone who knows taxes, who knows this and who knows that. Now I've discontinued using them by mutual agreement, because I told them initially that $150 a month for their services was all that I could afford. It was costing them much more. They are a great company and for three months they carried me; they wanted some of this experience too, I guess. They still do my taxes.

Too many beginner-entrepreneurs miss up on the vital need to understand what management is all about . . . it's the basic key to success. You can't just leave it all to the accountants and lawyers, can you?

No, because lawyers don't know anything about running the business. They have no idea about the operational headaches or the cash flows. Accountants are, for the most part, simply people who put on paper what you report to them and they're very careful to point that out to you at all times. But they can spot things at the end of the month or quarter and they can alert you to trends that may present future problems.

No, you have to wear many, many hats; you have to be willing to delegate but still keep an overall control. And this is the biggest problem for people coming out of an *employee* atmosphere. They aren't watching some of the things that are occurring and if they knew enough . . . had enough diverse experience . . . they could see it.

The first thing you must understand is that if you can't read a set of books, if you really can't understand how they're made up and what they mean, then you shouldn't get into any business. You have to understand books, you have to understand budgets, and you have to understand that you can't get emotional. If you say you're going to forecast this, then that's what you've got to do. I run cash flows every week here for three weeks ahead. You've got to manage your money. You have to understand money management . . . it's *your* money!

After you've assured yourself that you can manage money, get a going program. Know your market; establish what the market is; and for God's sake be sure that when you're establishing your share of that market, you establish it with the tools and resources you currently have. Anyone can look better if they get gold-plated stuff or whatever. That's always the way I ran plants in the big corporations. Just work essentially with what we have first and be successful with that. Those are the two or three things that I've found that helped me. Don't be afraid to change your program also, just use it as a guideline. We're happy with our program because we're way ahead of everything at this point. But don't be afraid to change one.

Also, you have to have the ability to understand the business. I had never even heard of a filter business before. So learn the glossary of the business as quickly as you can and rely on your ability to pick good people. You've got to have complete faith in your people.

When you're buying an existing business and if you're talking the price range you're talking about, you're not going to get much. The only thing you're going to get for that kind of money is, most likely, a business that is failing. If they're very prosperous, they're going to get a helluva lot more money. So when you buy an existing business, don't have any assumptions that everything is going to be there . . . in the figures that were *here*, they didn't have anything, which is typical. I think the only thing an existing business gives you is some contacts, which may or may not help you, and "good will," whatever that means. I don't believe in good will. By the way, I'm going to try and sell mine when I leave. Your good will may be good for you, but it may be terrible for me.

But you wouldn't discourage people from going into their own business?

No. But I would say this. You have to be willing to *take risks*. Look back over all your past history and first of all determine how many times have you really taken risks and was it worth it and how serious was it? Because one of the biggest is going into business for yourself . . . particularly if you've got the security of a permanent job with a check coming in . . . that's a helluva lot bigger risk than having children, getting married, buying a house, doing anything . . . and it's awfully lonely.

I've done a lot of sailing and after one or two races that I crewed on, I really felt that I knew sailing. One of the most frightening times in my life was when I owned my first boat after many years of sailing with people. I got out in San Francisco Bay and some trouble came up and I was scared. I *had* all the ability to take care of it but all of a sudden it dawned on me, my God, there's no one. I had always turned to someone before and even though I didn't ask, I knew that they were there to help me in case I got into trouble. I think that's the way it is with business. Most people have to understand that there's really no one there to help you. If you can live with that . . . and you must learn to live with that . . . you've got to get off and get going and you cannot alibi others or circumstances. You've got to say I've done everything I possibly could and that's it. You can't fault people.

Update

Passing through Tucson a couple of years later prompted me to call Ken Dean for a checkout of any new developments at Air Filter Service.

Result? Multiple shock waves! He wasn't there any longer. He had sold out many months before.

Wanting to know more, I hiked over to the present owners (at a new location) for a quick chat, and then continued on to the business broker who had originally been involved.

New Owners:

"We hear about him occasionally. He and his wife did split up, but that wasn't the main reason for selling. It may have been the culminating factor, not the reason.

"The last we heard, he was working for several companies who buy up businesses that may not be doing well. Ken gets them on their feet, hires people, sets up offices, basically trouble shoots their problems. He was in Brazil for a while, then Central Europe . . . all over, I guess."

Ken's former employee:

"I don't think it was an economic problem. It's just that there wasn't enough challenge for Ken. He said the whole operation got to be *too* routine."

Business broker:

"The new owners didn't buy the business from Ken Dean . . . there was another turnover before that. All in all, Ken had the business about ten months . . . he had it well organized and I kind of agree that it must have been too tame for him after that.

"Although his selling price wasn't much different from the amount he paid, there was a good hunk of profit in the turnover because he retained a healthy, well-built-up accounts-receivable position. That money coming in was his, so he did okay for himself. Ken was a darned good businessman. The person who bought from him only had it six weeks . . . it wasn't his bag and he quickly realized his mistake. But it's still a good growth business."

Well, there it is. Although Ken Dean is no longer in his first small-business venture, his original interview is still valid for the lessons it can impart. And, not to be forgotten, that initial venture turned out to be a very profitable entrepreneurship after all.

Measured by that standard, Ken did start and he did win in small business. Much of that success can be attributed to his analytical planning and preparation plus the actuality of a follow-through. In retrospect, if we reread his interview, it's easy to see that a Ken Dean might require a lot more activity than a simple distributorship could offer.

Success-Steps Analysis

It's really an eye-opener to see how getting started in a small-business venture is factually appraised and accomplished by a corporation executive, especially one who has worked in all the areas of production, marketing, and finance.

In Ken Dean's case, it was all there at the very beginning. Drive, leadership, analytical creativity, and the ability to communicate—the specific personality characteristics that have always proved themselves in any study of successful achievement. In and of themselves, of course, they are no automatic guarantee of success; it's how you coordinate them that counts. By adding business knowledge, sales and marketing experience, and a strong commitment, the long odds are with you.

When Ken decided to take the plunge, he moved fast . . . perhaps too fast for most of us. Since we don't know his inner motivations or how long he had been thinking about going it alone, the speed of the matter isn't important. What is fascinating, though, are the stepping stones his activities have laid out for us. They are a result of his strong business background. Many of these steps are perfectly valid for your own calculations.

(a)   He looked for a growth locale—target area, the Southwest.

(b)   An existing business was the choice, rather than starting from scratch. His past business experience would make it easier for him to analyze and project within an already established enterprise.

(c)   Type of business . . . any reasonable vehicle that would give a return based on sound management (14% return on net sales).

(d)   Before purchase, he analyzed the books and then wrote his own business plan and projection. These programs were then checked partially or totally with a friend, a bank, and a highly skilled professional accounting firm.

(e)   His analysis weeded out beforehand the area that seemed weakest . . . the manufacturing aspect.

(f)   He preserved his start-up capital by negotiating favorable terms for the purchase price. That, in turn, facilitated an immediate investment in fresh inventory.

(g)   Professional help was employed to set up the books and record-keeping needs from the very beginning of the new operations.

(h)   His projection included a growth of 15% in the first year. Increasing existing business could not be counted upon without some major extra effort or fresh approach. His new representation with the national manufacturer was applicable to both requirements, and successful.

(i)   Although the entire staff consisted of four people, Ken had formulated a program of personnel profiles, responsibilities, and corporate direction for the next three years.

Once again I must reiterate that the listed highlights are a direct result of Ken Dean's previous management experiences. In all fairness, the great majority of our readers will not have been in any position to have acquired this background. But that's the very reason I was determined to include it in among the interviews. Note also that every corporate executive does not a winner make. Many of them do not have a thoroughly rounded background in all the phases of management, but may have operated exclusively in sales, production, finance, or marketing.

Dean's "trouble-shooting" assignments in the varied industries always required an initial problem-analysis and eventually equipped him with many more management tools. But even with that, when the chips were down for his own business, he did not hesitate to engage an accounting firm to verify his projections and set up the operational paperwork. If that's a lesson to be learned, let's remember a few of the others that his interview suggests.

Make a plan, but don't be afraid to change it—it's only a guide.

You will have to take risks . . . but they should be the kind you've given plenty of thought to. Delegate authority, but keep an overall control. Understand what the books mean, what they say. Know your market and ensure that you get your share of it. Pick good people and don't ever get emotional about the business. And, about money management . . . remember you're spending your own money . . . making your own profits . . . taking your own losses.

The stepping stones as outlined, plus Ken's "program," constitute the major areas of a business plan. He finalized what his product would be, how he would procure it, the way he would market, the details of the "buy" agreement, personnel requirements, projected profit and loss statement, cash flow statement, corporate set-up and long-range goals. By looking at that kind of a total picture, the odds for making a good decision were considerably increased. If possible, it's a goal that every potential entrepreneur should aim for.

Although Ken Dean was interested in any business that would give him a good return, this should not be taken as a solid criterion. For you, on the other hand, may follow up on something you already know, have as a hobby, or select simply because it appeals to you. His admonition to not get emotional doesn't mean you should avoid a business you really like . . . just don't let your emotions blind you when the time arrives for clear thinking and hard decisions. After all, it's pretty clear that Ken is doing what he enjoys . . . "the business of business."

Business Plan: Ideal vs. Reality

Without question, a business plan serves to illuminate what you intend to do, how you intend to do it, and the way you intend to accomplish these objectives. Equally important it may also tell you to forget the whole thing because of obvious deficiencies that become exposed.

It's reasonable to ask, then, should the new entrepreneur have a formal, structured business plan to start his or her own enterprise? Most of those related to teaching, writing, or consulting in small-business management would shout an unqualified *yes!*

For instance, in buying a business as Ken Dean did, his thorough plan was an essential in determining what he was finally buying, how to identify his needs, market, and sources, and how to pinpoint specific returns and profitability.

Also, when approaching a bank, venture capitalists, independent investors, or even an SBA loan, the formal business plan is vital. For those ventures that require large start-up capital investments or expansion of an existing enterprise, there is little chance that anything will be done without it.

A business plan that I looked over recently was prepared for the purpose of seeking funds to expand and re-equip an existing modest operation. It was addressed to both a bank and the Small Business Administration and was set up as follows:

- Introduction   amount of loan and purpose
- Business Description   retail/wholesale/service
- The Market   customers, marketing area
- The Competition   direct and indirect
- Location   site, footage, lease
- Management   principals and resumes
- Personnel   job identities, salaries
- Application of Loan   capital purchases, renovations,
                                   working capital?
- Financial Data   capital equipment inventory
                                   balance sheet
                                   break-even analysis
                                   income projection—3 year pro-
                                      forma
                                   cash flow—3 year pro-forma
- Supporting Documentation

That's one example . . . about twenty-five pages. Other plans have included marketing strategy, research and development plans, and organizational charts. If this type of formalized business plan is a must for your project, then professional help will be necessary . . . especially in the financial projections.

The reality of the matter, however, is that only a very small percentage of the hundreds of thousands of small businesses starting this year will have any kind of plan, detailed, formalized, or other. The great majority of new entrepreneurs are understandably stymied in the planning area by one or more formidable barriers. Those stumbling blocks relate in part to the new entrepreneur's uncertainty about the future, his or her lack of knowledge and experience, the inexactitude involved. Some feel it's not worth doing because of a reluctance to devote the needed time and effort and, yes, others because of their super-enthusiasm which makes them predict super-success, thus neglecting the need for the required planning.

Well, if you intend to take the plunge into your own small business, all I can say is . . . do plan! Let's put aside the formalized version and let's forget the barriers. Take it one step at a time.

After you complete an honest evaluation of your personal resources and skills as a first step, start the next step by simply writing an outline of what your business is all about. For example, start with these basic questions . . . at this stage, you should be able to answer them easily.

What type business are you going into?
Who are your customers?
What is your total market?
Where is your market area?
Who are the competitors?
Why are you better?
How will you sell your product/service?
How will you manufacture or buy?
Who are your suppliers?
What kind and amount of space do you need?
Where will you locate and why?
What form of business—sole proprietor, partnership, corporation?
Do you need personnel? What kind?
Will your business be cash or credit?
How much start-up capital for the following?
  • equipment, furniture, fixtures
  • initial inventory or supplies
  • three months of salaries, rent, phones, utilities, general supplies, deliveries, travel, misc.
  • legal, accounting, insurance, miscellaneous fees
  • utility deposits, licenses, permits
  • initial advertising
Where will you get the capital?
Can you estimate sales for three months?

If you answer all questions thoughtfully, it will be the beginning of a workable plan, one that points the way and allows for the setting of future goals and timetables. With the help of an accountant on the financial questions and approximations, you may be able to project sales, costs, and profits for a year or two . . . subject to the inevitable changes that will surely occur.

Of equal importance, however, is the fact that even this informal, simplified plan will help you to develop your management skills. It will also alert you to the possible problems inherent in the areas of all these basic questions.

4
Starting from Scratch Again?

Peter Heineman, 27, has already been through the "starting-a-new-business" syndrome quite a few times.

After switching in college from business courses to science studies, he almost completed a degree in marine biology. Along the way he fell in love with the idea of a "lobster farm" . . . growing lobsters through artificial cultivation.

After a government grant, a college work-study program, and plenty of research at Scripps Institute of Oceanography, the potential for this idea proved to be highly unmarketable.

Then there was the actual business venture of raising *one-pound* shrimps! But, alas, there was no way to make that dream pay off, either.

So, what next? And . . . how?

HOMARUS, INCORPORATED
* MOUNT KISCO, NEW YORK

Imagination, enthusiasm, commitment . . . all are great ingredients to put into the magical entrepreneurial blender from which emerges the final choice of what type business to start.

The "lobster farm" idea was also speculatively attractive to Peter's dad, a public-relations executive, and to Richard Solomon, a former principal of Lanvin Cosmetics. They became a part of Homarus, Inc. as venture capital investors. On this venture, fortunately, the major loss only involved Peter Heineman's time and dedicated efforts.

The shrimp fiasco, however, involved the loss of Peter's time, his efforts, and a whale of a lot of his investors' money.

Let's start at the beginning, Peter. How did Homarus get set up?

I had read about John Hughes in Martha's Vineyard. He had a lobster hatchery, but his theory of a lobster farm sounded like a terrific idea to me. Once I talked to him and saw some of the things that might be done, I was hooked! That was it . . . I was all ready to go!

I talked to my dad about it and then to Solomon. They suggested forming a corporation . . . Homarus, by the way, is the Latin word for lobster. Then we consulted with John Hughes; I went to a lobster conference on the West Coast; I worked at Scripps Institute for a year to learn more about the lobsters; and finally . . . it was no go! One of the project leaders suggested I pick something else: "As it stands right now, you've experienced what we're up against . . . it just isn't going to work, not the way it stands now."

No large capital expenditures were required up to this point, is that right?

Yes. Homarus had money *if* the potential was there. If lobster culture was feasible, the money was set aside, in limbo, waiting to pounce upon that opportunity. It was *their* "venture" capital. I was putting in no money at that stage, but I had a seven year stock option to purchase my share of stock at the original investment price. I would have to pay my way into owner-ship, too . . . it wasn't going to be handed to me.

Actually, then, that wasn't the formal start of the busi-ness.

No, not then. But a short while later I followed up on a project that involved the cultivation of one-pound fresh-water shrimp. They actually do get to the size of one pound in nature.

This type of aqua culture was of interest to many large companies . . . Weyerhauser, Pepsi Cola, Coca Cola. They were, and still are, somewhat involved. There are the shrimp ponds in Hawaii, also. So this looked to be much more of a viable possibility.

There was this biologist with an ingenious scheme to grow these shrimp in plastic "condominiums," plastic cages, one set on top of another, with porous plastic floors whereby food would drop through to feeding platforms that were offset in each cage. He had some varied setups in his living room, as test samples, that indicated the potential and the feasibility of this direction.

To make a long story short, we gambled and went ahead in San Diego with a pilot project. We rented a house with a large land area; laid out a greenhouse 30' × 100'; fabricated 35,000-gallon raceways; built the plastic cages. There were two biologists, a botanist and myself, to get things going. And they went . . . after a lot of work . . . to *nowhere* that could prove out profitably!

> *This time, there was a capital investment. I know the project failed . . . but to what extent?*

Once we realized that the economics weren't right, it *all* went down the tube. Also, my associates were typical researchers with all that the term implies. "More money is needed" was their constant battle cry, and sound business practices really had no bearing on their projections. It was a complete failure to the tune of a very substantial initial investment . . . almost six figures.

Biologically, it could work. But not in any cost-effective way. Because one of the biologists wanted to keep trying, I turned the whole shebang over to him for $4,000 and traveled back to the east coast. After travel expenses and paying off the accountant, Homarus only had five or six hundred dollars left.

> *Now what? Did you think of getting a job with someone else or was being in your own small business the only job you ever wanted?*

I always found it against my grain to go to work for someone else. I always resented authority, even in school. I just can't see myself working for a boss and having someone watch over me . . . I would much rather keep my options open and go into business for myself. Even with our present business, however, I look at it right now as a small business, but I don't want it to *stay* a small business.

To get back to your question . . . no, I didn't want to get a job and, at the same time, I wasn't going to stand still. The one aqua culture aspect that was a proven business was raising trout . . . twenty million pounds a year are raised in the U.S. A quick survey, however, proved that it would be too costly in the east because of the need for hydro pumps to maintain the tremendous water requirements that are the major component of a large trout farm. In Idaho, for example, one farm that I visited raised three million pounds of trout without the need of a single pump . . . it was all handled by gravity feed from the springs. Try competing with that!

Once burned, your evaluative judgment gets a lot sharper. What was the thinking that got you started in the present venture?

After three years of hard work and frustration in California, the thinking still seemed to stray in the direction of "things fish." Accidently or on purpose, we started experimenting with a small smoker that dad had purchased as a gift for my mother, who is a gourmet cook and authority.

We tried smoking cod and whiting, and all kinds of fish, as well as trout. Man, that trout was really good.

So we bought some more trout . . . it was readily available. We brined and smoked it up and took it around to a few local restaurants and they said all right, send in a couple of dozen. And I said to them, wait a minute, I can't send them in, I'm just asking you if you like it. I realized that I'm right back in that same syndrome of . . . they're saying yes and I'm not able to produce it. So I stopped immediately, right then and there, and I built a smokehouse in our backyard that could produce about 150 fish.

But you had to dig up the know-how for that . . . it wasn't something you were familiar with?

No, not then. But everything's a learning process . . . even going into your own business. That first smokehouse wasn't a super-professional one and we had to figure out the plumbing, the sources for supply, the best smoking time, and so on. Karen—we weren't married then—worked with me from the very beginning.

Once the first smoker was built, we started to experiment with the brine. That's when the brine really went through its change, right there, right at the beginning. We began to use a lot of spices . . . trying spices and *not* trying them, using brown sugar versus white sugar, using different concentrations of salt. Finally we evolved the special brine we have now. It's a unique combination that helps give our trout a distinctive flavor and keeps the flesh firm.

There were lots of other problems we had to lick. We ruined a lot of fish trying to come up with the best way to hang the fish so that they would process properly. The heat had to be just right . . . hot enough to get through but not enough to shrink the flesh. You would have laughed to see us out there with flashlights at night, checking the smoke-house process or hanging the fish for a morning order.

Anyway, we started taking them around to local country clubs and restaurants and began putting together a few accounts. We were up against it moneywise and Karen tried to get a job nearby so as to generate some capital . . . but that didn't work out.

Karen: So I became a fish saleswoman and hopped the train to New York City with my box of samples . . . "tasting samples." I was a little nervous, going to some of the big and famous restaurants, knocking on the door, going in the back, and trying to get the chef to taste the trout. It was pretty tough at first, but it's a lot easier now.

Peter: Things *were* becoming a little better . . . we got a few good breaks here and there. I think we picked up Tavern on the Green and Four Seasons around the same time. Then we got the Waldorf to take some. So we began to generate activity . . . we had reason to feel optimistic for the future. And I began to draw a very small salary.

Was all this from the backyard smoker?

Right. We were turning out maybe 200 fish a week at this point and we bought a small freezer, so that we could store the fresh frozen trout from the Idaho fish farms.

Karen and I were constantly out selling and in late August I thought we should build another smokehouse, so I did. Our capacity, then, at any one smoking, was 300 fish. So we started to really solicit some more accounts. We picked up La Caravelle and Le Poulailler restaurants in New York, as well as a few more local ones. I'd say our volume at that time was 300 or 400 fish a week.

In late November we took time out to get married and take off for a while.

Then we went into January and February . . . mind you, this was all done outside now and that winter was a real, real cold one. We used to freeze ourselves out there, hanging fish up. Our fingertips would be so blue, we'd turn the burners on and get down and warm our fingers. It was all done from my parents' cellar and backyard, where there was plenty of land so that no one was disturbed by the smokers. We would have to carry the fish from the cellar out to the back garage where the smokers were. We had a station wagon and I'd load the back of the wagon and back it all the way up to the smokehouses and then later cart it back in and then we'd pack the fish and then we'd load up the wagon and take it in and deliver them. In New York, Karen would sit in the car so it wouldn't get towed away, and that would be that.

It was a real partnership, then. Was Peter's Whole Smoked Idaho Trout starting to pay off?

The partnership was from the very start. We froze together and went through the whole shebang together. At that time the expenses were just the cost of the fish, really, because we had no overhead . . . we were in my folks' house. Now we were really starting to get the framework of the business together. We had a fairly good billing procedure and we were making fish on a regular basis and we had our own Homarus telephone put into the house and were buying some decent equipment to process fish with. We re-did one of the rooms in the cellar to make it look pretty sharp and we cleaned it up. At this point in time, we were starting to really think that we had something that could support us and, hopefully, make us rich.

Then we began looking around for a facility. We looked and we looked, because the minute you mention smokehouse everyone thinks they are going to get smoked out. We were turned down in many places, and the prices for rental were prohibitive for the volume of business that we were doing. Nothing seemed right, so we abandoned the idea and we just kept doing it out of the house for a while. In the spring I built a *third* smokehouse . . . just in time.

That's when we got our first big order. I can remember it as if it were yesterday. We supplied 500 smoked trout to the Waldorf Astoria for a big party, and because of it we also got the business of a very large caterer. We really started to roll then—April, May, June; June was our biggest month. We now had about 25 accounts, which included many of the finest and most well-known restaurants in New York and the suburban areas.

At this point we went to Richard Solomon with June's figures and our progress. He gave us the high sign as far as *his* interest was concerned, as far as buying a building and really doing it right, because he realized that we had taken a business from *nothing* and were now generating $8,000 a month.

This meant that fresh capital would now be coming in again . . . your dad and Solomon as stockholders and investors?

Right. The same original setup . . . with no fabulous returns, as yet. When I got the go-ahead sign, I looked for a few months and finally found this building. After some haggling and negotiation, we took it over. There were two or three months of renovation . . . you wouldn't believe the work involved.

Meanwhile, we were still turning fish out of the backyard. Then we moved in. The first two months were terrible . . . in January and February we did $10,000 worth of business, that's all. We really were hurting because we only had trout. We had no salmon yet. I had bought 1,000 lbs. of salmon and didn't know how I was going to make it. I had a cold smoker built for the salmon, but it wasn't lined with sheet metal, so I spent the month of January lining it myself and getting it ready. Then I began to pursue getting recipes for Scotch-style smoked salmon. I didn't want to join all the others who were supplying Nova Scotia-style salmon. So I got hold of some Scotch recipes and I added my own touches once again, and I also got the idea of pressing the salmon to get that firmness, instead of just letting it soak in brine.

I gather that the pressing isn't normally done. What made you go into salmon?

No, the pressing is not normally done. We went into salmon because man cannot live by trout alone (chuckle). In other words, we had to expand because now we had an overhead. One of the things that alleviated the problem, the real pressure of overhead, was the fact that we rented part of the building back to the original owner for his showroom space. That basically covered our mortgage. By doing that, we didn't feel the need to come up with mortgage money and any slack in sales could usually be taken up by not paying ourselves much, so that way—I won't say we could break even, but it would sure help alleviate any losses.

You're now getting past the strict do-it-yourself stage . . . much bigger investment all around. How does it all shape up now?

The cost of the building was no big secret. We paid $150,000. I've got a $100,000 mortgage. That was when Dick Solomon and my dad came back into the picture. They put up the initial money.

The equipment was added as we got money, as we *made* money. A year ago, equipment-wise, this place had just the bare essentials. I would say the original equipment investment when we got into this building wasn't more than $12,000 or $13,000. We just got by; we had whatever it took to make the fish, but nothing more. Now we have roughly about $25,000 worth of equipment. I'd say we have about $10,000 worth of refrigeration and we just had a new smoker built. We've gotten a load more of processing equipment, stainless tables, shelving, and accessories.

But when we first got into the building, it was still a do-it-yourself operation. Karen and I did it all . . . preparing, brining, smoking, filleting, selling, taking orders, packing, delivering, and invoicing. When things weren't busy, Karen would just grab a box of fish and salmon, go into the city and solicit business from places we would predetermine. She did some selling, all the bookkeeping and managing, while I handled all the production, maintenance, and sales.

It took me a while before I got salmon down to where it should be. I had humidity problems that I didn't realize I would have, because the salmon should dry properly. I had problems getting the filleting done; it's very difficult to fillet a side of fish properly.

When you're talking $50 a fish, you don't want to screw that fish up—one wrong cut and you shave off $10. Salmon is cold-smoked, which can take anywhere from 12 hours to three days, depending upon the humidity in the air and the size of the fish. The trout is something else . . . it's warm-smoked and four hours can complete the process.

Anyway, we worked damn hard and we're still doing it. But now we have some help . . . Fred Baker joined us a few months after we were in this building, and his son-in-law came in a short while back.

The interesting thing about the smoked-fish business is that the amount of space necessary to produce a tremendous amount of stuff is very small. We could produce about 1,200 trout a day out of here, out of this cement building with the existing hot smokers, and easily 300 sides of salmon a week. Now a side of salmon is five or six pounds and the selling price, at this time, is $6.50 to $7.00 per pound . . . that's not bad.

Do you have any salespeople? Or is advertising the answer?

We're the salespeople. We cover New York City and the suburbs. We send a truck into New York every day. A lot of business comes in on its own now, just from referrals. And we keep in touch with all our good friends . . . the chefs. The personal touch is necessary and, at the same time, we enjoy it. As a matter of fact, it's very important that *I* still do the delivering every once in a while . . . to keep in touch. They almost get angry at you if you don't show up.

We do have a distributor in Boston, Turner Fisheries. They're a Tiffany outfit . . . they charge more than your usual fish distributor but they have the best quality and one of the best air-freight delivery systems I've ever seen. That's why we took them on for national distribution. There are certain places around the country that have heard about us, and now our fish are in Missouri, Vegas, Kansas City, and all over the place. We even ship to Bermuda and the Caribbean.

The only real advertising we do is for our Saturday retail sales . . . we use the regional newspapers, Penny Savers, and the local Patent Trader. Otherwise, PR has been very good to us with feature articles in the newspapers, magazines, and an occasional mention here and there. You really can't beat the exposure you get from public relations.

Retail sales? Are they meaningful to your operation?

And how! Because you get the money right then and there, you don't have to wait for it, and you don't have to go through the expense of billing it. It also gets rid of . . . in this business you have a lot of seconds that are not 100 percent perfect. You'll have a beautiful side of salmon but it might have a blood spot that was done by some fisherman when he caught it. So you cut that blood spot out, but then you can't sell that side to a restaurant even though it's a perfectly good piece of fish. These we can dispose of to the retail consumer, and with the amount of salmon that we're now making, it's very important for us to have those Saturday sales.

There's another advantage, too. Our retail business keeps us in touch with the marketplace. Lets us know what our product is doing . . . getting better, getting worse, what is acceptable, if it's too salty, or not sweet enough, et cetera. It becomes a valuable barometer.

You and Karen started from ground zero . . . how have the sales grown and what do you see for the future?

In a few more months we will have completed our third year. Roughly, the first year we grossed $60,000 in sales, the second year about $250,000. We hope to hit the $500,000 mark by the end of the third year.

Our sales at this time are split 50/50 between the trout and the salmon. So it was a good gamble to expand with salmon. But it was an even bigger risk, after the salmon seemed to be moving well, to order 50–75,000 pounds of salmon for the future! I took a real chance then . . . but if I didn't, it would have been worse and now I'm lucky I did.

What about the future? I think fish is in! It's becoming one of our main protein sources. Those who usually turn up their nose at fish really relate to *smoked* fish . . . because it does change the taste completely.

We'd like to get into mail order and perhaps even expand internationally. What I'd like to do is begin to be a trader in the seafood commodity market. If you know what you're doing, and you know what you're buying, and you know the stocks that are available in the ocean, and you know the quota systems that are going to be imposed by various governments as to the amount of fish to be taken, you can make a lot of money in buying various types of seafood such as shrimp, salmon, halibut, and the specialty seafood items.

That's big money again . . . and getting back to that factor, how is the corporate setup relating to all this? What about your ownership?

The original corporation was set up as a Subchapter S corporation. We all knew the speculative and research aspects of the beginning pilot projects . . . so we would be losing rather than making money.

We're now changing from the Subchapter S to a regular corporation, so that we can begin to accumulate working capital. Last year we had to distribute the surplus to each of us . . . then we paid tax on it and then we put it right back into the business as a loan, because we needed that money to work with. This is the last year that's going to happen.

At the same time we're right in the middle of negotiating exactly what stock participation I'm going to get, what Solomon is going to get, and what my dad is going to get out of it. But I—or I should say, Karen and I—will be the major stockholders.

All in all, it's been a good partnership and I hope it gets better. I'm happy with what we've done . . . an incredible amount of hard work, sure, but I see it as a means to an end. The time when we can get the business to the point where it runs itself . . . you know what I mean. It really never does, does it?

No, not to the point where you can let go. Ease off, perhaps, but that's about it. In line with that, what about your competitors?

That's an interesting point. I really never did any research on them originally. If I had, there would have been no Peter's Smoked Trout or Salmon! If I had seen the quantities they were making (one sells almost a million pounds of smoked salmon a year) I would have been overwhelmed and dwarfed . . . it would have made me feel that the project was futile.

Now I don't want to know what or how they're doing it . . . it might influence me or structure me into some kind of conformity.

I take nothing for granted anymore. I never think an account is sewed up.

My attitude is that I'm just about to lose them. I strive for quality and people will pay more if its better. And your buyers will go for the better quality . . . to protect their own reputations and to satisfy their own pride.

Success-Steps Analysis

The Peter Heineman interview offers actual behind-the-scenes insight into a great number of questions that have to be considered by every beginning or potential entrepreneur. Some of these are:

- Is starting your own business right for you?
- How do you choose the type of business?
- How do you determine product selection?
- How do you actually get started?
- Do you need a marketing strategy?
- What about growth and expansion?
- What about capital? Risk?

Getting fired up by an idea or a unique approach to an idea is certainly one way to start off with a bang. Couple that imagination with enthusiasm and some dedicated effort and it's easy to see the attributes of success really building.

But Peter showed us that there's a lot more that's necessary. Both the "lobster farm" and "shrimp condominium" required additional research before they could be considered practical. And that word practical means much more than just feasible or possible . . . it also has to mean positive cost-effectiveness and profitability, without which there will be no business, big or small, to worry about.

Interestingly enough, if those projects had been possible, each would have required a good deal of additional capital for actual production via artificial cultivation. And what about need? Was there sufficient demand for one-pound shrimps? For cultivated lobsters?

The point is that all of this analysis and probing should be a part of your selection of product and business, whether it's a new invention, a manufactured product, a service, or a retail store. Practicality, market need, ability to produce, capital, profitability . . . weigh them all, so that your risk is a calculated one, not an out-and-out gamble.

Also, going into business was obviously Peter's thing. He had the absolute desire to be on his own . . . in fact, that actually proved to be the only "job" he ever had. The drive was there and the total immersion of effort to the task at hand is quite evident in the learning processes he had to go through.

It wasn't surprising that Peter Heineman stayed with thoughts of "things fish" and something that involved his own personal food tastes. Many a venture has been started exactly that way, by relating to things you know, have as a hobby, are interested in, like to do, or stumbled upon accidently.

His steps, this time, reflected some of the wisdom that was assimilated from his previous projects. Peter's Smoked Trout was based on an accepted product; a taste difference was added; samples were tested; the ability to produce was determined; the market was identified; the start-up capital and technical requirements were modest; and his home base helped to make it all practical.

It wasn't a cultivated or manufactured product. The trout were shipped directly as needed from the Idaho fish farms . . . already cleaned, eviscerated, and ready for smoking. That made figuring out cost-effectiveness and profitability a lot easier, especially when it also involved all do-it-yourself labors.

Growth and expansion were carefully controlled . . . smokehouses #2 and #3 were put up and used in the backyard. Operations remained in his parents' home, and all the increased sales and output were still handled by Peter and Karen. Only when his product was proven and the increase in accounts reflected this, did Peter think of larger, physical quarters . . . and the need for additional growth capital.

His "venture capital" was already a part of Homarus, Inc., and that was fortunate. But his proven track record and books may have enabled him to procure an ongoing business loan. Acquiring the building and the later inventory of 75,000 pounds of salmon certainly required "big money" and this will always be the case when your small business starts to make the crossover into something bigger than a "his-and-hers" operation. A lack of working capital at that crucial stage has strangled many a small business.

With the addition of an overhead factor, (the new building and expenses versus his parents' home) it made good business sense to increase his market by adding a new product line. Product acceptability was the risk. He already had the necessary refrigeration, the physical space, packing and shipping facilities, and the same marketplace as a potential for salmon sales. All that was really needed was a cold-smoker and the ability to produce a more desirable product, one the market would respond to.

The added outlet of a retail sales unit was also an excellent marketing move, and so was the special effort to retain the personal contact with his accounts, especially the original ones who helped start them off.

Fortunately, also, the thinking hasn't stopped there! The Heinemans strongly relate to the business guidance that can be offered by their accountant, lawyer, and most particularly from their fellow stockholders —Peter's dad and Richard Solomon. Additionally, serious thought has been given to other areas of activity . . . mail order and perhaps commodity buying in the seafood market. Planning ahead, while still conducting an existing business, is a definite plus! It's the kind of bonus that pays off in the future and it usually results from acquiring or developing a "business sense."

All in all, the prognosis for this third phase of the Homarus "saga" appears to be one of "full speed ahead." Both Karen (who was not available for most of the interview) and Peter are completely bullish about the future of the company. They expect more hard work ahead—and some greater rewards!

Sources of Capital

Equity Capital: (Monies to start business)

Let's face it, most would-be entrepreneurs have the idea that banks and the Small Business Administration (SBA) are the money sources to get them started in their own small, new business.

Without doubt, banks and savings and loan associations are in the lending business. But, fortunately for their depositors, the loan risks they undertake are normal and fairly well documented. New businesses do not fit that category! They fall into the high-risk arena and the very structure of banks prevent them from taking such unusual risks.

Exceptions? Sometimes. If the new businessperson is putting up 50 percent of the required start-up capital; if they have a good credit rating; some management experience in the type of business being started; and can show a good business plan . . . well, then the bank may be willing to become involved. Don't blink your eyes on that one . . . not when you consider the tremendous rate of failures that result from poor management of new ventures. Banks will go for a calculated risk, not an out-and-out gamble!

Okay, you say . . . let's go to the SBA, who will guarantee 90 percent of the bank loan in their bank-participation loan program for small business. Here again, it isn't that simple. First, you have to be turned down by the banks before you can apply to SBA. Secondly, the forms and requirements for that bank-participation loan aren't very much different from the bank's own application forms. Both these factors are the reason why only a small percentage of SBA loans, direct or bank-participation, are related to start-up capital for a new business. Most SBA loans relate to existing businesses with needs for working capital, expansion, et cetera, that already have a track record that can be documented. Exceptions do exist, however, but they are made with specific programs that are directed to the economically disadvantaged and minority groups.

In the meantime, let's get back to those realities that concern locating the money necessary to start a new business . . . your own small business. If you are willing to lift your head out of the sand and take an honest look, these are the usual sources of that start-up and equity capital:

> personal savings, investments
> personal loans (signature or co-signers)
> life insurance loan
> home mortgage—second mortgage or refinancing
> relatives and friends—loans or investments
> credit union—if you are a member
> sharing ownership—active or silent partners who will invest in the
> new venture

The final listing—sharing ownership—can also apply to the more formal sources, like venture-capital companies and small-business investment companies. Their procedure is to supply money in exchange for stock ownership in your business. Although this is also equity capital, they are not looking for amateurs! Their interest most often concerns well-run small companies that are ready for growth and expansion, or new situations based on some exclusive idea, product, or service. They themselves are usually highly professional and can offer strong management, financial and marketing support. For this reason they will be listed in a later category.

Working Capital: (Monies to run the business)

As the business starts to function and grow, the everyday running of that business will require ample working capital. These are the short-term funds needed for inventories, payrolls, and to carry your accounts receivable. Part of that comes from the cash generated by the business and the remainder can be obtained through short-term loans, as well as specific applications of capital conservation. Many of the sources that could not help with start-up monies are available for working capital loans:

> commercial bank loans, credit lines
> credit union loans
> commercial finance company loans
> accounts receivable loans
> warehouse receipt loans
> factoring of accounts receivable
> extended trade credit from suppliers
> leasing instead of outright purchase
> merchandise on consignment
> SBA loans—occasionally for working capital

Growth Capital: (Monies for expansion and modernization)

Loans for growth capital most often relate to the purchase of fixed assets and are usually long-term. Generally, the purpose involves business expansion, modernization, or some significant change that will result in greater levels of profits and cash flow. This growth capital outlay may bring about increased sales, cost savings, or greater production efficiencies resulting, perhaps, from the purchase of buildings, equipment, or modern machinery. More than likely these long-term loans will be secured by using some of the company's fixed assets as collateral.

Sources for growth capital financing often overlap with those used for working capital, but the rationale and repayment periods are obviously completely different. Additionally, this is the category where government agencies and private financing companies that cater to existing businesses can be listed. Their loans and investments in these cases usually relate to expansion and growth, or additional equity capital.

> commercial banks
> life insurance companies
> leasing companies
> mortgage lenders
> sale and lease-back agreements
> SBA loans—direct loans
>   bank-participation loans
>   disaster loans
>   economic opportunity loans

state and local development companies
Small Business Investment Companies (SBICS)
Minority Enterprise SBICS (MESBICS)
private venture capital firms
family venture capital firms
Economic Development Administration

The Small Business Administration (SBA) has approximately 100 offices throughout the country. Check the one nearest you for information on the SBA loan programs. Your local commercial bank may also be able to supply the necessary information.

For information on Small Business Investment Companies (SBICS), one source that will be extremely helpful is the National Association of Small Business Investment Companies (NASBIC), 512 Washington Building, Washington, DC 20005. Send for their free 21-page directory booklet, which explains venture capital, SBIC financing, and lists about 300 member companies with their names, addresses, loan limits, and type of business preference.

5 Partnership—Yes or No?

Partnerships are most often thought of as twosomes, but they can really comprise any workable number of participants.

They can be structured as a partnership form of operation, or if desirable, as a corporation.

Joanne Fiala, Pat Heanue, and Kathy O'Connor, all in their early thirties, chose a corporate structure for their first entrepreneurial venture.

Results, after three years, indicate it was a formidable combination . . . . a true example of strength in unity.

VANTAGE CAREERS, INC. ★
WHITE PLAINS, N.Y.

Vantage Careers is an employment agency located in the city of White Plains, approximately twenty-five miles north of metropolitan New York.

One of the trio, Pat Heanue, was not available for this scheduled interview . . . and with good reason. She had just delivered a new baby girl the previous day and her associates, Joanne and Kathy, vouchsafed that everything was under control, both at the hospital and in the office.

Partnership is often a questionable blessing. In your case, how well did you know each other before starting the business?

Kathy: We were friends for a long time . . . . it's been years and years.

Joanne: We went to high school together. And, although we wound up at different colleges, our friendship continued. Then, by being in the same field of business, there was an additional bond of interest:

70

*One of you must have been the motivator for starting a
business. What were the circumstances?*

Joanne: Our missing partner, Pat Heanue, was the one with the idea. She and I had discussed it a few years before, but the timing wasn't right. Financially, at that time, I wasn't able to take the risk and Pat wasn't under any real compulsion to start up. There were ample reasons to make the move when we finally did get together.

Kathy: Pat had a newborn baby and wanted to work no more than three days. Doing that for someone else was a problem, so she felt the best thing was to work for herself. She had the background to make a go of it, so it was plausible. However, to go into it with one or two other people would certainly make it easier all the way around—she wouldn't have to start with an absentee management, particularly at the crucial beginning stages.

Joanne: We all had small children then. Pat with her new baby, I had a four-year-old, and Kathy's daughter was seven. For my part I couldn't work full-time either. I needed a situation where the hours could be lessened. So Pat and I had a couple of phone conversations and then we approached Kathy to see if she would be interested.

Kathy: And . . . my situation. The company I had been working with had recently been bought out. Although the new team coming in was fine, I wasn't really happy about it, so I was looking for a new opportunity. Fortunately, our needs seems to mesh and I guess that was the beginning impetus for our business start-up.

*You all were experienced . . . was that in the same area
or with the same companies?*

Joanne: We each had about six years' experience in personnel placement and we were all geared to the secretarial—clerk—non-exempt type—positions. Anything in the support level is non-exempt. Not managers. All it means is that if you work overtime, you get paid. Managers don't.

Kathy and I were working for different agencies in White Plains . . . in the temporary-placement area. Pat also started that way but she later developed a permanent-placement division within her agency group. That kind of experience was extremely valuable for our business because Pat was the one who had done it before . . . actually built it up from scratch for her previous employer.

Were there any other individual strengths . . . different areas of responsibility that could complement each other?

Kathy: When the new group came into my agency, I was manager of the office and I had to work a bit with their budgets, their figures, and their bottom line. Among the three of us, I was the only one who had any financial knowledge . . . but only up to a point. Even with that we were all weak in it, definitely not the strongest point for any of us.

Joanne: I had handled temporary placements for a while. Then I got into sales and I was on the road, knocking on corporate doors. Pat, as we mentioned before, was in permanent placements. Each of us had similar, yet different experiences.

In our industry, contacts are all-important. Not only with the personnel managers of companies, but also with an applicant following. This means the people in the community who come to you or refer others to you because they know you're good at placing people. So when we did combine forces, we also combined three sets of contacts. That's what the business is all about. It really was a great help in getting started.

That was the thinking behind it all. How did you actually get started? The initial capital, location, et cetera?

Joanne: Like anyone else, we thought to get some professional help. We asked someone, who today is our insurance broker, about a recommendation for an accountant. We went to him and he drew up a financial picture that was presented to the bank for a loan. The bank didn't turn us down, but they didn't say yes, either. They wanted more information.

Kathy: None of us had any large savings, or stocks, or other goodies . . . the things they always want to see. But our accountant helped us with financial statements of our personal possessions. Only Pat owned a house, which was probably our largest asset. Then he indicated our expertise in the field and how it was a continuing situation, not just on some willy-nilly basis. Our expenses for the first year were projected and, based on previous experience, we also showed what we anticipated for our initial year's operation. It wasn't too formal, fairly casual, but quite informative.

We were looking for half our needed money from the bank, providing half on our own. With all the added information and some prodding from our accountant, the bank agreed to the $10,000 loan. But we were asked to sign personally for it.

Joanne: Yes . . . and it was a pretty stiff interest rate, too. You know the bank's philosophy. They say, "Forget the high interest rate. Just remember, if it's too big a risk, we don't even want it!"

Was the total of $20,000 enough to start up with? Did you need any help besides yourselves?

Kathy: Well, what we were supposed to have done was to add our $10,000 to the bank's $10,000 loan. But we decided we should go in on a shoestring . . . use the bank's money and at that point not take any salaries for ourselves.

Joanne: The accountant was actually horrified that we were going to start a business with that little money. And, admittedly, $10,000 was considered pretty low to go in with.

Kathy: Sometimes you can't listen to too much professional advice. Don't forget, we weren't taking salaries and the only one on payroll was our receptionist. We needed her right from the beginning.

Our space, on the third floor of this building, was only about one third the size of this . . . a little over 400 feet. A reception area and a few offices for interviews, et cetera. It wasn't a big outlay, like a store with lots of stock and fixtures, or a manufacturing operation with raw materials, machines, and all that.

How does a service operation of your type physically get going? Where does the business come from?

Joanne: We advertised that the three of us were going into business, and we sent an announcement out to all the contacts from our three lists.

We had incorporated in November and opened our doors in January, so we had six weeks to prepare ourselves, set up our schedules, review and compare our lists, and make some early contacts.

After our announcements had gone out, we started follow-ups by phone. As soon as we had a few job listings, we advertised in the local classifieds for applicants. From that small beginning, those same factors start to multiply. More listings, more ads, more applicants . . . and finally, the building of a good reputation.

We were not neophytes. We were professionals in our field. But it was our first time on our own and we were apprehensively feeling our way.

Kathy: We were able to take salaries in the fourth month we were in business . . . small salaries. Pat, Joanne, and I worked as counselors . . . interviewing, evaluating, placing, sometimes negotiating. The three of us and our receptionist were it! Then in the sixth month we brought our first counselor in to help out.

Did your original thought on timing work out . . . one of
the reasons you all got together?

Joanne: In a way yes. I varied between four and five days the first year. Pat, with her newborn, worked three days, and Kathy worked four days.

Kathy: Sometime after the first year we added a bit more solidity to our setup when we were able to hire Ethel. She was a counselor who had been in business for 10 years, was extremely well known, an excellent person in this field. Her schedule was a full five days.

Also, at that point we felt the administrative work had really increased. That instead of being fully productive as counselors, we were getting more and more involved in building up sales and handling operational details. That's when expansion started to rear its welcome head, and we began thinking of more space and more people.

Expansion can be healthy if the results are there. How did
the first year stack up with your projection?

Kathy: I think the first year we expected to do between $70 and 80,000 gross billings. In actual fact we outdid our own expectations. We went right into six figures! You just can't believe it.

Although you do have confidence when you start a business . . . and certainly no one expects to fail . . . it's still a pretty big question mark. But, even so, until you see it . . . seeing is believing. That first year we were very excited.

Joanne: A year and a half after our modest start upstairs, we took our present space. Our entrance is from the lobby area now, which makes it more convenient for applicants and those who may be curious about what's around in the job market.

You can see what we accomplished with our architect. There's a large reception space out front with two enclosed areas for typing and transcribing tests and brushups. We have a place for coffee and refreshments, a private office, a large area for the counselors and their interviews, another office space for overflow—and all of it is fairly well appointed.

Yes, it feels and looks professional. At this stage, how many counselors do you have and how are they compensated?

Joanne: There are nine people besides ourselves. Eight of them are counselors. The only person who's really salaried is our receptionist . . . and she has the hardest job of all.

In our field of work most agencies have their counselors on a commission basis. A few may relate to salary and a very small commission, but we've always found that anybody who's really good would rather work on commission, because they make more money.

I'd say that generally the counselors get a commission of 25–40 percent of their actual gross sales. It really depends on the philosophy and experiences of each agency.

Speaking of other agencies, didn't you have competition when you started?

Kathy: When we opened three years ago, we felt there would be two who would be our strong competitors. Where Pat had worked was one of them, so we had a little edge there. The second we felt would not hinder us from growing, simply because there was room in the field and business was starting to really come into White Plains . . . a definite growth situation.

Joanne: One corporate park after another started to come in. We just happened to hit the perfect timing. Not only were large companies coming in, but there also were our major shopping areas, with Bloomingdale's, Sears, Macy's, Saks Fifth Avenue, Bergdorf's . . . lots of new restaurants, specialty shops, French bakeries, and you name it.

We don't relate to placements in retail. The point was that all this activity spelled growth. White Plains was becoming a small central city in the widespread Westchester area.

Didn't that booming growth bring in competitors . . .
not too long after you had started?

Joanne: Well, many have come and gone. Recently, this year, there are many new ones. But, again, I think it relates back to the fact that the three of us had been in this area a minimum of six years each before we started. This area and this field. We know this town and that's been extremely helpful.

Kathy: You'll get agencies from New York City who feel it's a good expansion move for them to come to White Plains. What they don't realize, sometimes, is that it's a very different market. We grew up with it and when it exploded, we were here! It's still kind of a social, small town in its own way.

Obviously things have gone well for Vantage. Have you
kept up the first year's pace and what do you see in the
future?

Kathy: Thankfully, yes. That first year's success has multiplied a number of times and we're now in a very comfortable six-figure gross. Our salaries, based on time, are where they should be and there are equal-share bonuses, too.

We have plans for opening a branch office in Stamford or Greenwich, Connecticut. We've been sitting on that for a while, doing surveys up there. It's probably a year away.

There are a great number of personnel agencies up there.
How will you break in? Pirating?

Joanne: There certainly are. Stamford is one agency after another.

But we've already advertised for job applicants in both the Greenwich and Stamford papers, so our name is known, and we're not going in there as a total "new guy on the block." Also, between the two areas are some of our very good clients and they would also be clients and contacts when we get to Stamford.

Kathy: You mentioned pirating . . . no, we never did that here in White Plains. What did happen was that our reputation grew. When we advertised for a placement counselor, people from local agencies would respond. If your reputation is good, you end up attracting some of the best people in the field.

We're going to adopt that philosophy in Stamford. After opening an office, we hope to attract some counselors who may know or would like to know about us. It's the same principle as we have here . . . where contacts are very, very important. It's not like opening a boutique where people are walking past, they like what they see, and come in to buy.

To digress a bit . . . since you are all mothers, I'm
curious as to what got you started on careers. Was it to
supplement income or to further express yourselves?

Joanne: For me, it was a combination of both those things. I know I could never be the type of woman who could just stay home, five days a week, with a small child. So when my child was very young, I only worked two days a week and my situation was in sales. Subsequently my husband and I separated and the income has become more important to me.

Kathy: When I first began working, it was almost strictly to supplement income. My husband was in grad school at night. My child was eighteen months when I went back to work full-time, and I found that difficult. As she got older, it was a bit easier.

I used to be the first one to say, "Oh, I could have stayed home and had five children." Now, given the total freedom of option, with money no longer a problem, I just feel I couldn't go back at this point and be the total housewife. I'm still too involved with other areas of expression.

But I am expecting my second child in a few months.

Joanne: Pat at that time had no children. Her oldest now is three and yesterday she had her second. I think she wanted to supplement income, to buy a house, to have a few things they both wanted, and to wait awhile before having their first baby. Also, I guess, she wanted to take on a challenge, too . . . out of the house.

With Vantage . . . were there any negatives along the way? Especially at the beginning?

Joanne: Oh, little things, perhaps. Basically we've had pretty smooth sailing. Particularly during the first few years, which people say are the most difficult.

We've come to realize that we couldn't depend completely on professionals . . . not as much as we thought. Because we thought they were all-mighty in their fields, we relied on them a little too heavily. Some of our own feelings and instincts were sometimes as good, if not better, than theirs. We had to learn to be a bit more independent of other people.

I think our most difficult problem was our first expansion venture. We were actively going into the professional placement area. Perhaps because we didn't put the time and energy into it that we should, we've had a lot of problems with it.

Kathy: We incorporated that area under a new name . . . Westfield . . . and we have office space in this building. I guess our problems stemmed initially from the person we hired to start this unit's operation.

It was a new field for you. Often that in itself can create problems. Are you continuing it?

Joanne: Yes, and that's a perfect example of working in an area that's not your normal cup of tea. Again, you kind of do what you know best. We didn't know the higher professional level as well as we know the clerical and we didn't have as many contacts.

I think, once again, relying on someone you think is knowledgeable to manage another area . . . well, it just didn't work out. That person had a whole different philosophy than we did as to the type of placement we wanted to do.

We certainly haven't deserted the Westfield concept, we're going to continue it. But I think we're going to continue it with Vantage as the base. We have gradually been getting into higher-level placement with the counselors we now have. We're growing with it, we're moving with it.

Kathy: Somehow when you first start out, if you have not had that many dealings with the professional people . . . which none of us have had . . . it's a lesson to be learned. You just kind of feel like this is their specialty, so I can let them handle this part of it . . . that's not the way it goes. We now have only one person operating through the Westfield name, in the data processing area. It's growing with her and eventually we'll move someone from here also.

> *Getting back to the idea of partners or people working together. There must be many factors that have to mesh to make it a good thing.*

Joanne: I would say one of the key ingredients that has made us work so well is that we all trust each other. I think that is very, very important in any kind of partnership situation. And it's complete, total trust!

Kathy: We trust each other as far as the books are concerned, the people we hire, the decisions we make. That, more than anything else, has made us a good working unit.

It wasn't a casual acquaintance, where you can think you're good friends and have a lot going for you, so you get into it. It's like living with someone. You spend more time at work, particularly when you're starting a business, than you do at home. You can easily compare it to a marriage.

Joanne: Another thing that was good with us was that we found we were different personalities. We each appealed to different kinds of clients. The people that like Pat didn't . . . they didn't necessarily dislike me, but they had stronger feelings toward her than for Kathy or myself. That factor, the pooling of the lists of different clients and applicants, really launched us so quickly into a good first year.

How do you partition the work? Is one more of a boss than the others?

Joanne: What we try to do, since all of us now work in an administrative/sales capacity, is try to rotate the jobs among the three of us.

For example, one of us does sales for six months and the other does purely administrative work. Then we rotate, not just because of trust, but to give each of us an overall view of the company. When we all come together for meetings, each one of us has experience in the different aspects of the company. I'm convinced this makes the decision-making process a lot easier. Because you've been there; you've done it.

Especially in our industry, where we work so closely with our counselors. At some point or other, one of us wears the sales manager's hat. And it's important for each one of us to experience that day-to-day contact with them. What's their production? What are they doing well? What are they doing better? What are their problems?

We have a check system on Friday, where we talk with each one of the counselors individually. We rotate that among the three of us as to who's going to do that for the particular week. They're really the bread and butter of our organization and if they're not producing, we're just not making any money, and neither are they. When we come to a meeting together, if one of the counselors has a problem, we're all aware of its meaning and the necessity to help in the resolution.

Kathy: Each one of us has a little more expertise, or a little better feel, or more creativity in a certain area. We do tend to sort of take over those areas a bit more . . . if it's mine or Joanne's or Pat's.

However, by rotating our responsibilities, we really do get the overall feel of the business and it's easy to fill in for one another in any area. Otherwise, if you're not at all involved in other areas and if one person is the expert there, you would be relegated strictly to their opinion and decisions. That could make for possible problems in any business.

You've all done a great job in three short years and I'm impressed by the professionalism of the operation. By the way, are you working night and day to keep up?

Kathy: No, we still claim very flexible schedules. But I think if it really came down to punching a time clock, we'd find that we're spending a lot more time than we realize. We don't spend a 9-to-5 day week, but frequently we've had meetings till eleven at night.

Any time there are major decisions to be made, we all meet in the nighttime or on a weekend. Any time there's a crisis, there are always additional hours.

Success-Steps Analysis

The major impetus for starting Vantage Careers was an interesting and somewhat unusual set of motivations.

Pat Heanue, who initiated the idea, needed a situation that did not involve a full five-day work week. Joanne Fiala also wanted to lessen her work days, and Kathy O'Connor, although not unhappy in her present job, was ready for a change.

Here again we pick up on the beginning of a series of positive moves that led to a very successful small business. In coming together and forming a partnership, they joined much more than a trio of hopes and dreams. There were distinct assets:

- they each had needs that could be satisfied by a merger of their time and talents
- they were friends of very long standing and knew each other's personalities well
- they all had good professional experience in the same industry
- their choice of a business was limited to the exact field they worked in
- they each possessed different client contacts within that field
- they were all willing to accept the risk factor and the initial struggle

When you examine assets in a partnership, this listing assumes great importance. Participants in a partnership often wind up disliking one another; getting involved in heated controversy; almost coming to blows when angry; distrusting each other; and even cheating one another. Often, real emotional pain is inflicted.

Consultants have indicated that most often potential partners spend a lot of time evaluating their occupational backgrounds. They investigate what each can bring to the partnership in experience, contacts, and industry knowledge. Although that is certainly important, it is vital that equal importance be given to the personality and compatability factors. That's where the trouble most often starts and that's where knowledge about one another is usually the weakest.

Pat, Joanne, and Kathy were fortunate there. Being continual friends since high school gave them an insight into their personalities and how each might react to the rigorous demands of a partnership, which means constantly living and working together, as in a marriage. They would also be aware of any personal crisis or deep-seated problem that might interfere with each member's total commitment to the venture. Apparently, this basis of their compatability is existent and flourishing . . . three years' worth, so far.

Their business itself shows up some interesting facets also. Normally many partners select one another for the different skills each can bring to the merger . . . i.e., sales, production or administrative strengths. In the case of Vantage Careers the three had essentially the same thorough experience in personnel placement, although the slight differences of emphasis were extremely useful. Because of the type of business it was, these almost-negatives became positive assets.

The strength of the personnel business is centered heavily in the client-contact area. Because they had all worked primarily in actual placement and/or client soliciting, the merging of their individual contact lists became the invaluable starting point of the whole operation. Add to that the fact that their business has no capital machinery investment, no inventory, no shipping and distribution, no product, and no services requiring any of the above . . . and ergo, there's the positive again.

The usual requirement of different skills was not vital in their case. Management and administrative techniques, on the other hand, could be acquired along the way, with growth. Of greater urgency was placements, and all three could concentrate there . . . exactly where all their skills existed.

The singular demands of their operation also explains the "getting by" with lower-than-usual starting capital. But, in addition, by beginning with a just-as-much-as-we-need modest office space and no salaries for the partners until they could afford it, they avoided the mistake of many an overly ambitious entrepreneur. Their bank loan, incidentally, was repaid in six months.

The Vantage expansion was a direct result of increased business rather than wishful thinking. At the same time, they took advantage of professional help in spatial design and decor for the new offices. The look is very professional and adds to their image of competence in the field.

Other experienced counselors were added, as the principals themselves spent more time in the administrative and sales areas. This type of flexibility and strengthening of changing directions indicated that management is not just letting things run quietly along. There's planning at work, new strategies being undertaken, and no fear of necessary revisions.

Pat, Joanne, and Kathy were all involved there. Their trust in each other, their different personalities, their professional knowledge, and the interaction of these elements apparently worked for Vantage Career's growth.

The mistakes of the professional placement division did not go unheeded. It was a lesson and it was absorbed. The decision was to strengthen it internally and develop it with the slower pace of increasing experience in that field. A branch office in Connecticut is being evaluated carefully, but part of the groundwork for it is already being put into place, in the event a go-ahead is finalized.

An idea that is really meaningful is their rotation of responsibilities. If each partner can be somewhat aware, by actual involvement, of all facets of the business, then the decision-making process becomes more democratic and much simpler.

Many a partnership has floundered on the abdication of responsibility by one partner to another . . . "because he knows more about it." In some cases it happened willingly, in others it may have been enforced. Carved-out areas of responsibility often create dissension, because of a lack of understanding and communication between the principals.

At Vantage they realize they're a team . . . all playing in the same game and all wanting to win together.

So far . . . excellent!

One additional thought that made lots of sense was using the corporate form of organization for their joint venture. It limited personal liability. In the event any of the partners drop out, the sale or transfer of stock ownership is facilitated. Similarly, if new partners need to be added for growth and other divisions, both talent and capital are more easily obtained with the corporate setup. Finally, the business has a continuous life . . . it is a legal entity, able to be run by managerial personnel in the event of sale of stock or death of a principal stockholder.

Forms of Business Organization

Many factors come into play when deciding what form your small business should take. Whatever the decision, however, keep in mind that it's an initial choice, especially if it's a sole proprietorship. As business needs and conditions change, you can also convert the organization into a partnership or corporation.

As a first venture, there are some clarifying questions that may help determine which form to choose:

- Starting capital. Can you handle this yourself or will you need assistance from someone or some source that has funds available?

- Management. Do you want to have complete control over decisions, direction, promotion, or other matters? Is that why you originally decided on a business of your own?

- Know-how and skills. Is the nature of the business such that you can manage, sell, and produce or do you require partners—each with a specific and complementary skill? Is it a business solely dependent upon your own services?

- Jeopardy. Does the business place you into the area of great personal liability which can result from claims, debts, and damages against it? Is there danger of personal injury to clients or customers?

- If you become ill or unable to work for a period of time, do you want the business to continue?

- Taxes, forms, stock, regulations, et cetera. Does this kind of paperwork and detail stymie you, and will it distract you from the commitment of concentrating on the initial business start-up?

Add a few other questions that pertain to the type of business you are contemplating and the resultant answers will inevitably point to a specific form that should be chosen. As a beginning, let's review the most common legal forms of business organization.

Sole Proprietorship

The easiest organization to form. An individual who starts this way uses his or her own, or borrowed, capital, and is solely responsible for whatever goes on in the operation. At the same time the sole proprietor has total personal liability for any claims, debts, or lawsuits that may arise in the conduct of the business.

Legalities are simplified. A certificate of doing business or a fictitious name statement may be the only formal requirement necessary . . . it is usually filed at the county clerk's office. The need for licenses or permits for a specific type of business should also be checked.

Income taxes do not require that special business tax forms be filed. The business income (profit or loss) is taxed as personal income and is entered and computed on the individual's own Form 1040, Schedule C. It is then added (or subtracted) to other personal income. Sole proprietors also must pay a self-employment tax for social security coverage.

If the owner cannot continue the business, or is deceased, the venture must cease and all aspects of the business are to be concluded.

The sole proprietorships are the oldest form of business and the 1970 census indicated that they comprised over 75 percent of all firms. Although there were over 9,000,000 proprietorships in the country, they were responsible for only ten percent of the total sales.

Partnerships

The census showed this form of organization to represent 8 percent of all firms, close to 1,000,000 units. It accounts for only four percent of total sales. Partnerships are, however, one of the older forms of business and their beginnings related, most likely, to the early formation of family units.

Although we often think of partnerships as involving only two partners, this business form can and often does, involve two or more people running the business. They may have equal shares in ownership or some partners may have more than others.

There are two kinds of partnership, however . . . a general partnership and a limited partnership. In the general form, all partners are equally liable for any claims or debts relating to the business. This is an unlimited liability and involves each general partner's personal assets, in fact, any one partner can involve all the others in a responsibility for claims or contract terms.

In the limited partnership, investors can become partners without incurring unlimited liability. They usually are responsible only for the amount of their original investment. This should be indicated by signing a contract agreement, and by filing a special certificate. To use this form of limited partnership, however, there must be at least one general partner involved.

Most partnerships are in the general format and usually start because of the need for a combination of skills. This may involve partners who have available capital resources, or who are each proficient in a specific business aspect, production, sales, finance, or management. Partnerships are also easy to set up . . . usually with the registration of an assumed-name certificate and any licenses or permits required by that type business.

Each partner is taxed on his or her share of the partnership income at the personal-income tax rate. Paperwork is a bit more complicated in that the partnership files a Form 1065 with the IRS with a Schedule K-1 that shows the shares given out. A copy of that Schedule K-1 is received and filed by each partner, by being attached to his or her own Form 1040, where the partnership income is then added to other personal income.

Although not required by law, it is imperative that a written agreement between partners be set up with an attorney. It is advisable to spell out all the details: shares, duties, responsibilities, capital investment, buy-sell, and termination procedures. Legally, death or withdrawal of a partner does terminate that partnership, but a new contract or agreement can keep the business going within another arrangement.

Corporations

The last census indicated over 1,500,000 corporations, and while they represent only 14 percent of all firms, the corporations accounted for 86 percent of total sales!

Strangely enough, not only big businesses use the corporate form.

Small, and even one-person firms, have chosen this organizational format as the best way to fit their needs. Admittedly, it is the most expensive to set up, requires the most paper work, comes under the most regulations, and is more costly to run.

A corporation is a legal entity with its own identity as a legal "person." The owners of this form of business become shareholders and employees of the corporation. As such, the owners usually are not liable for claims against the corporation . . . where special circumstances do indicate personal liability, it is limited to the amount of their original investment.

From the time of filing articles of incorporation with the state, to the final dissolution of the business, there are more paperwork, regulations, and costs than with any other forms. Compensations do exist . . . shares can be sold to raise capital, the corporation does have a continuous existence, the liability of the owners is limited, it's easier to attract people with needed skills by offering shares, and it's easy to transfer ownership via shares.

Taxes are more complicated, with specific corporate reporting forms for federal, state, and local agencies. If dividends are declared, there is a double taxation involved . . . the corporation pays taxes on profits and the dividends are then taxed when received by the stockholder.

Because it is the most complex form of organization, it is advisable to use an attorney to initiate the corporation.

The *Subchapter S* corporation is a version that combines some of the advantages of a partnership and a corporation with relation to the tax situation. It is a corporation legally, but it avoids the filing of corporate tax forms. It files, instead, an information return with the owners paying the taxes as personal income. An attorney and accountant can clarify these aspects.

WHAT FORM OF BUSINESS ORGANIZATION?

SINGLE PROPRIETORSHIP

ADVANTAGES

1. Low start up costs
2. Greatest freedom from regulation
3. Owner in direct control
4. Minimal working capital requirements
5. Tax advantage to small owner
6. All profits to owner

DISADVANTAGES

1. Unlimited liability
2. Lack of continuity
3. Difficult to raise capital

PARTNERSHIP

ADVANTAGES

1. Ease of formation
2. Low start up costs
3. Additional sources of venture capital
4. Broader management base
5. Possible tax advantage
6. Limited outside regulation

DISADVANTAGES

1. Unlimited liability
2. Lack of continuity
3. Divided authority
4. Difficulty in raising additional capital
5. Hard to find suitable partners

CORPORATION

ADVANTAGES

1. Limited liability
2. Specialized management
3. Ownership is transferrable
4. Continuous existence
5. Legal entity
6. Possible tax advantages
7. Easier to raise capital

DISADVANTAGES

1. Closely regulated
2. Most expensive form to organize
3. Charter restrictions
4. Extensive record keeping necessary
5. Double taxation

Source: SBA's Starting & Managing Series, Vol. 1, 3rd edition
"Starting & Managing a Small Business of Your Own"

6 Combining Two Businesses

Thirty-two year old Janet Ramey was familiar with some aspects of running a small business. But her previous ventures were quite modest by comparison to the present operation.

With her very good friend and partner, Laurie Allen, they pooled their knowledge and unrelated backgrounds to come up with a completely new wrinkle in a highly competitive field.

Along the way, much additional learning was involved. One costly lesson encompassed the very familiar need to "get it in writing." When her contractor went $8,000 over his estimate, she sorrowfully wrote on the check, "tuition."

BLUE WILLOW RESTAURANT AND POSTER GALLERY * TUCSON, ARIZONA

Although most people think the business failure rate of restaurants to be one of the highest, this is no longer true.

The president of the National Restaurant Association, Thad Eure, Jr., comments, "Running a restaurant is a complex task and a risky undertaking, even in the best of times . . . but restauranteurs are getting better ideas about how to run their operations and this is obviously a major factor in the lower failure rate. This improvement is one of the strongest success stories in the economy."

The Blue Willow is situated in an older house, with a parking area, on North Campbell Avenue. This is a long, busy main stretch that contains a great number of restaurants. Many are fast-food franchises, which run the entire gamut . . . burgers, tacos, doughnuts, fish, chicken, and all combinations of same.

Janet, the idea of a poster gallery and restaurant is fabulous. While I waited for a table, I joined all the others looking at the cards and posters.

That's the idea. It was a mob scene this morning, but it's Mother's Day . . . this one woman looked at me and said, "Did you expect this many people?" I said, "We always expect a crowd, because we always have a crowd . . ."

The combination idea makes our waiters a lot happier, too. The people who are waiting for tables have something to do instead of sitting there, drumming their fingers and thinking, "God, it's been twenty minutes, already . . ." When they do get seated by the waiters, there's no pent-up grumpiness.

Another benefit is that after people have eaten, they must walk through the gallery to the cash desk at the front. Invariably, they browse on their way . . . pick up some cards, perhaps.

Simple question, then. How did it all come about? What was the thinking behind a better restaurant idea?

Mainly we were looking for something that Tucson needed desperately, and that was a good place to eat omelets. There were no good breakfast spots around that were moderately priced and had real good food and some real alternative food.

I think people are scared these days of the word "alternative," because it could mean anything. But what we mean is *real food*. We have four different kinds of fresh fruit just as a garnish on each plate and we make every order up individually. We go to a lot of time, trouble, and effort to make the food both real and good. It's the key to our success . . . the success key for anybody in the restaurant business. It all starts with the quality of your food.

Was a specialty of omelets so novel in Tucson?

Well, there's that and more. We have 22 kinds of omelets. Also, people can make up their own. They can have anything they want so long as they can find the ingredients on the menu somewhere.

We make all our own soups right here. And salads, four types. Then I personally do all the baking for the restaurant, which keeps me going. We have five desserts every day, of which one is the specialty of the house, our "chocolate du jour." Both my partner and I are "chocoholics," so we had to get in one of those.

There are also sandwiches, granola, yogurt, avocados, quiche, plenty of cheeses, espresso, cappucino, fresh fruit juices, and lots of other wonderful goodies.

We took a chance and got a beer and wine license. Neither of us is a drinker, so it was a little unusual to do that. But the idea of a fresh spinach and ham omelet with a glass of wine and a chocolate mousse for dessert was just mouth-wateringly good . . . so we did it. It's worked out very nicely. We were afraid we'd attract an element that we weren't enthusiastic about, inebriated customers, but we haven't had any of that at all.

The combination of businesses to highlight the restuarant wasn't just a lucky hunch. There must have been a great deal of thought behind it. Why that choice?

Mostly because we hadn't seen it done anywhere and we wanted to do something that hadn't been done before. The uniqueness of your ideas is a real key to being successful. So find an idea and give it hell and see if it works. If it works, you've got a winner. If it doesn't, you can just leave town.

True, but it does have to depend on your surroundings, your locale. It might not work everywhere.

Yes, it really does relate to your specific location. That's something everyone tells you all the time and it's another one of the key issues. You have to have a good idea, but it's got to be good for your location. If there are already a dozen omelet places, then having an omelet place isn't such a hot idea.

In the long run you have to offer a quality product and you have to present it uniquely. You have to find your market . . . try to find a spot that isn't overkilled down the road. That's a hard combination, one you've got to think out and research.

Why the gallery part of the combination?

What's happening is that the graphic world is going crazy these days. The graphics that are coming out of the West coast and the East coast are just *phenomenal*. The card lines . . . if you told me a few years ago that I was going to be having a card shop, I would have thought of nothing but little old ladies with flowers and Hallmark cards. Nobody that *I* knew sent cards to anybody.

But now, wow! The graphics in cards are just great . . . especially the beautiful things coming from the West coast. Then there are the quality art reproductions in poster form. You can get a Fujita, or a Gustave Klemp, or a Breugel for six dollars!

You can afford to put one on your wall and look at it, yet you don't have to be involved in a huge investment. You can own something that is a quality piece of art work for very little money. That's what's appealing.

The combination works. You saw it in action yourself. People love to browse when there are beautiful things to look at. On the way in, on the way out . . . and especially while waiting. We've also added some wonderful boxes, earrings, crystal, and calendars, as companion look-see items.

Your background was the restaurant business. Does your partner relate to the poster gallery area?

Yes. Laurie Allen, my partner, owns the huge bookstore just up the street. She's had plenty of retail experience and she has a fantastic eye for what's going on in the gallery—for the kinds of things that should be there. Everyone is responding favorably to what she's done.

I've had two previous restaurants, both on a much smaller scale . . . almost on a coffee-house scale. This is a much bigger venture than I was familiar with. And yet those smaller ventures were the things that gave me the experience and know-how to tackle this one. This is a really big one for me.

Were you and Laurie long-time friends or is this purely a business arrangement?

We've been close friends for a long time and she's seen what I've gone through with my other ventures and has helped out as a friend. Laurie originally wanted to back another restaurant for me, but we got involved in this combination poster gallery-restaurant and then it got so crazy, that we've both spent much more time in the kitchen than anyplace else.

We trust each other completely and we both make decisions all the time, even in each other's speciality. Either one of us can make the decision right on the spot. There's no sense in her dealing with the broken dishwasher and me dealing with the broken dishwasher. *One* of us can deal with the problem there and the same with the poster gallery. We both carry the same weight and we both work in each of the areas, so we do know what goes on.

The reason our partnership has worked out so well is because our friendship has worked out beautifully. Nothing that happens here at the Blue Willow is more important than our friendship. It is the main event. I think that's what makes our situation so unusual. I can't tell you how many people I know as partners who have in one way or another dumped on each other . . . even husband and wife combinations.

Is Laurie active here? Does she have time from her bookstore? And what about your family situations?

Laurie still runs her book shop, but she has an excellent staff of people with her. She's also the top book appraiser in town. But, active . . . yes, she's helping out here all the time.

You should have seen her this morning . . . she was whipping those omelets out in the kitchen with the best of them. We both put those aprons on and run around here all the time. And I'm behind the desk in the poster gallery every day, for a little while.

We're both single now but we have been married. Laurie's also in her early thirties and she has a daughter and I have a young daughter . . . so it really keeps us moving. You have to have the ability to put your own personal life aside for a while, especially the first year. That's hard to do if you have a three-year-old.

Janet, although you and Laurie have had previous business experience, I'm sure there were many things that came along that were new.

I'm rolling my eyes . . . you can't get *that* on tape, but, yes I am rolling my eyes. M-a-n-y things came along. But we stuck with our original premise of inexpensive, quality food . . . real food . . . and they just jam in because it really is made here.

The public has been hyped for so long. Homemade pie is the old No. 10 can of pie filling opened up and then the old pie shell is shoved out of the freezer and dumped in and it's "homemade." But, it's not homemade! It's canned! Most of the public has been mouthwashed out of quality . . . they think cake mixes are the real thing.

The Health Department wouldn't let us use little jam jars on the table so we serve individual packets. Everybody else has sugar water, mixed fruit jelly . . . but we have the best quality, *real* blackberry jam in the single serving packets. It costs us more and people don't realize that, but we know it. If you price it out for your cost analysis, you just have to add that quality in. That's what people like.

Cost analysis is essential to any business. You must know exactly to the penny what every carrot stick costs or you won't know what you've got. You try to keep your overhead down, which is hard to do. You work a lot and your partner works a lot. That's a good part of it.

What about the hours . . . and the staff?

We're open 8:00 AM to 10:00 PM, seven days a week. We're committed to being here the full seven days. A lot of restaurants are closed one or two days a week, but we feel that people want good food all the time.

We have about thirty people working for us. Now we're able to hire people who are recommended by other staff members. They already know what it's like and they pass the word on. The first words out of my mouth are, "Are you hyperactive?" If they are, they'll fit in perfectly. If they're the type who has to do only one thing at a time and it has to be just perfect . . . well, they won't work out. In The Blue Willow, you have to be able to really move.

We're hiring older people all the time. We prefer late twenties and early thirties. They're more stable, have more mature judgment, and they usually stay longer. Younger people tend to move around a lot.

Our wages are high because we want a good staff . . . and that means the dishwasher, too. We have a free food policy for the employees. They may eat anything at any time, unlike in many other places, where there are special menus, leftovers, or restricted times to eat.

You mentioned cost analysis before. There must be plenty of administrative and management details here . . . keeping track of bookkeeping, waste, and markups.

Some of that does involve the big words . . . like the idea of "cost analysis." All that finally means is that you take each item on the menu and figure out to the penny what it costs you, and then triple it . . . or whatever you decide to do. Most businesses triple or quadruple their item cost or menu cost.

We don't have too much waste in our business because it's just too rapid a turnover . . . we can barely keep up with the ordering. There is some waste, of course, and it will show up by your food costs rising some percentage points.

If you don't do your own bookkeeping or if you don't have a real good hand on it, then you don't have a really good idea where your money comes in and goes out. You must have those figures in black and white.

You must say, "All right, my food costs this month were 35 percent and last month they were 40 percent. What or why are they 5 percent less than last month?" Is it because the staff has changed? Are we feeding less people? Is there more waste? Are basic costs rising?

You have to figure that out. It's important to know these things. Guessing just isn't good enough. Knowing also gives you good buying potential . . . you know just what you have to spend. It's also important because in a business like this you constantly put your money back into the business.

Then you have a bookkeeper here . . . where you can keep up with what's happening?

Oh, yes. We had a part-time bookkeeper here from inception. Unfortunately, we were so harried just trying to stay open, just trying to meet the unexpected volume that we started with, that it took our full energy. Our bookkeeping for the first six months was just a shambles.

She was a qualified person, but she had a nervous breakdown three months after we opened and she had a bad time of it. Because we were so busy, we didn't have any chance to look at it. I'll tell you, that will *never* happen again. I will never be involved in another business where I don't know exactly what's happening.

You must know! You must know exactly where your dollars are coming in and where they're going out, because your total source of income is what comes walking in the front door. That's all you have to work with and it's a definite amount. All improvements, all expenditures, all raises, bonuses, and all everything comes from that money. It has to be managed correctly or one day you don't end up with the right balance and you're over the hill before you know it.

Is it okay, now?

Yes, now it's very tight, and it will always be that way. The next time I do a business, I definitely will have my bookkeeping straight from the very beginning. None of these paper bags full of receipts that you go through six months later.

Our accountant did originally set up the books, but we were struggling and had very little money. We set up a very primitive bookkeeping system because, frankly, we had no idea we were going to have the kind of volume that developed.

Now we have another bookkeeper and we love him. He's great . . . he's perfect. He just walked in off the street. He's 68 years old and just exactly the balance we need. Someone older, someone who had a lot of experience . . . and someone who was willing to clean up our bookkeeping from the hectic first six months.

He will be full-time until we're caught up and then he'll be part-time. We will now do it all ourselves and the CPA will be in for yearly taxes.

It's a large operation and you're whole-heartedly involved. What does that mean, in time?

I wouldn't even begin to count the time I put in. It would scare me to figure out the weekly hours. I'm here before we open and I'm here a lot after that.

One of the key things about going into your own business . . . you have to have a built-in work ethic that's completely different from the way most people view their work situation. You have to be willing to do anything to make it work. Willing to sweep the floor, do the dishes, do 14-hour shifts and come back cheerfully to do another 14-hour shift.

You have to be able to do it all, because the person who owns the business is the one who sets the tone. If you want a restaurant, or any business, to be a quality place with people having a good time and working right along with high energy, the only person that's going to make it happen is the one who owns it. Nobody else is going to be as committed as you are. Nobody! You can't buy that kind of commitment, so you really have to be able to work.

Let's go back to the beginnings. Did you have professional help? Venture capital? A business plan?

We had a lawyer, an accountant, a real-estate agent, and we had a lot of friends who've been very supportive.

Financing is one of the toughest parts of getting started, and I can remember my first venture in San Francisco. There I applied for a loan from the Wells Fargo bank and they point blank said that unless I was from a disadvantaged ethnic group or handicapped they had no money for me.

People say there are small-business loans around but it's not that easy. You have to back your own venture and if it means starting off with a smaller project until you can get enough money for the bigger venture . . . then that's what you should do. You just can't count on anybody else coming through.

They also tell you that enough capital is essential . . . you must have back-up capital. Well, they're right. We bounced a check the first week. We were so short of money that we actually ran out. The bank called and said, "Gee, we hate to tell you this, but . . ." We had to rush over there with a few extra dollars to put in. Thank goodness the business took off from the very first day.

Did you have a bank loan to start with?

No. We each put up $40,000 from our own savings and previous ventures . . . selling my house, and so on. We thought we had enough money, but there were many delays and screw-ups with the contractor. We even started to do a lot of the work ourselves when we saw we were going to run out of money.

Anyway, that's water under the bridge. We did it without any bank money, which was really better for us. We don't owe anything now. Having a business like this, free and clear, except for the mortgage payments, which the business pays for . . . that's phenomenal.

To be open less than a year and both be taking substantial salaries, plus both to be making a living is very unusual.

It surely is. Did you take salaries from the beginning? And what about your business plan . . . how did that go?

Yes, we did take the salaries. We thought it was essential for our energy. I wouldn't do this for free, I can tell you. If there wasn't going to be any money made, I was willing to forego salary for a while . . . but as it turned out, we did make it.

Of course, as owners, our salaries have to be flexible things. If things go bad, the owner is the first one to be cut. But salary is important . . . if you go home after an 18-hour day and you have no money, but have to write out paychecks, it can be very depressing. If *your* energy is not up, no one else's is going to be.

As for planning, there was a lot of that. We knew what we wanted to do, how we would like to do it and where, the kind of people we wanted to attract, both as customers and staff, and a rough approximation of costs.

There again the key issue is anticipated volume. You don't know what kind of volume you're going to have . . . what to expect. And *all* your business projections and costs are based on the volume. So you have to guess. Even our accountant couldn't help there because he didn't have the expertise in that. Anticipated volume or yearly gross became the big guesswork on which all our other figures rested.

Did you outpace your initial year's "guesstimate" and get into the beginnings of six-figure volume?

Oh, yes. Way over. You wouldn't believe the amount of business so far, and it's just about the end of our first full year. We didn't expect anything like that, nor the tremendous amount of time and effort that Laurie and I have had to put in; but that's all part of the game.

After paying off all startup costs and taking substantial salaries, has there been anything left over?

No, not in that sense. Any time there is money left over, we just improve the place. We did the parking lot recently. Then the constant upgrading of equipment and renovation of the physical plant itself takes up every penny. We have a list of things we'd like to do next.

Because we have been successful, it makes it possible to use any "leftover" monies for upgrading the business. All our equipment is paid for, all our opening costs are paid for, and it really helps our peace of mind that we don't have any huge debts outstanding. The mortgage on the land and property are there, of course, but real estate is going up all the time and that will take care of itself in the future.

Where did you have some of the initial problems? I can't believe everything started smoothly.

Well, Laurie found the actual building and we were able to purchase it and then make major renovations. But it's a lot harder to renovate than build. I had to tie in a whole new kitchen with funky old plumbing from some forty years ago, which wasn't any picnic.

Here I designed and built a kitchen that I felt would be bigger than I would ever need . . . and it was too small the second day after we started. Believe me, that was a blow. It became a real hassle. We needed a bigger kitchen and we needed a connection between our storeroom and the kitchen . . . but we didn't have it.

Then we were really committed to having a hardwood floor, because they're beautiful and they're unusual. They give a whole new tone to a place. There was a wood floor under a layer of tar, and some ten other layers of linoleum going back maybe fifty years.

We spent weeks and weeks scraping this mess off and then hundreds of dollars to renovate the wood. Result? Well, some ideas start out as terrific ones, but in this case we ended up with a restaurant that's much louder than we would have liked it to be. So that one didn't work out too well.

The major equipment I put into the kitchen was not adequate and was not all brand new . . . after all, we wanted to start out slowly. That was a mistake, after the fact. We've had repairs but they've been manageable. If we could have known how successful we were going to be, I would have gone with all new equipment.

What type of clientele did you finally attract? You're not too far from the University of Arizona . . . does that have an effect?

We've been really fortunate because we didn't get any one group of people . . . all students or all retirees. We have a very big clientele of professional people, particularly at the lunch hour. There are a lot of family people on weekends, and since we're between the foothills and the university, we get a lot of professors, doctors, and other hospital personnel.

We have a younger set of people that comes here also . . . it's been one of the really nice aspects of The Blue Willow that it does attract everybody.

On this one street, from one traffic light to the next . . . how many restaurants exist?

Fifteen! Fifteen restaurants on this block. The day I counted that up, I said we must be crazy . . . this is really stupid. But what's happening on this street is that it's all your franchised, pre-packaged, pre-prepared food. All of that is so different from what we're doing, that it's given me confidence to keep doing what we're doing because it does work.

People *do* show up for quality . . . even if they have to put up with a little less than the perfect, stainless-steel atmosphere they usually see.

Yes, actually your decor here is very casual. What's the seating capacity of The Blue Willow?

It is casual, but that's also what's nice about it. Officially our capacity is fifty, but we now have added our outdoor seating, so it's going to be more than that. Maybe another fifteen or so.

It usually takes a long time for a restaurant to become known. How did you handle that . . . with advertising? A big opening promotion?

We opened later than we intended because our contractor was so late in getting finished. June was our debut. In Arizona, *nobody* would ever open a business in June. It's hot . . . it's a real stay-at-home siesta time for most of Tucson.

As it turned out, however, it was a stroke of genius because there was nothing else happening and we got a slew of free publicity. There were articles . . . radio . . . television; everybody wanted to talk to The Blue Willow owners because there simply was nothing going on in Tucson.

So, sometimes the thing you think is going to be the biggest problem turns out to be to your advantage. All that publicity was a great short-cut to people being made aware that we existed and where we were located.

Being an owner of a business is always a touch-and-go situation. Surprises and disappointments all the time.

Right . . . and that does happen constantly. You can never be sure of anything. I think that's the hardest stress for an owner, to get up every morning, full of energy, never knowing if it's going to be a breeze or not.

Everybody else isn't an owner . . . they know what they're going to find when they go into work. They may have a big work load or a small work load, but they usually know what they will be facing.

But as an owner, *never.* You never know what's going to happen. The employee who gets pregnant; the ones that are upset; the employee who didn't make it because she's stranded in the desert with a broken-down car; the dishwasher that fizzled out; the $1700 you spent to fix the parking lot and there's a big puddle there after the rain. You just can't pre-plan everything. You have to be willing to get in there every day and hope it works. It's exhausting!

And there's the public too. A lot of your energy goes in that direction.

It's new every day. It really is. It's very difficult to work with the public because you have to be "on" all the time. In a restaurant, especially one with a fast turnover where people are in and out in an hour or so, you are in the front lines all the time.

Maybe that's the 500th omelet you just made, but it's the only omelet they're going to eat and if it's not exactly right, that's the only thing they're going to judge you on. To give that kind of quality to absolutely everything you do involves a lot of stress.

Janet, your situation is the only one of my interviews that relates to so many employees. Are there other negative aspects to that kind of relationship?

It's hard, because if you're the boss, you're in an isolated position. It doesn't matter if your 30 people are outstanding people. It's hard to be friends or have personal relationships.

Since I'm a single woman, I definitely would not date or get socially involved with the people who are working for me . . . other than when we're at a party and having a good time together. Everybody thinks you have masses of friends and masses of good times and invitations, but it's really an isolated position and you have to be willing to accept that.

You know, being an owner isn't a personality contest, either. It's hard work to stay honest and direct and open with your employees, and not be too friendly or too unfriendly, too distant.

Once you cross that line . . . between sort of the cottage industry of single ownership to one having a number of employees . . . you're in a different bracket. It's a more stressful situation because you feel cut out of a lot of advantages and yet, you are the owner. If you're a sloppy owner, you'll have a sloppy business. That's what it boils down to.

It's amazing with all the negatives that anybody ever goes into it.

You're right. It's in the blood though, especially the restaurant business. I love it. I love to make good food. It's probably my own insecurity of not having had enough to eat as a child or something. But whatever it is, I enjoy it. I love having all this food around, putting it out and seeing people go "Oh," when you set that plate down in front of them with the fresh strawberries and the watermelon, the cantaloupe and the grapes, the whole-wheat and raisin toast, most of which they get along with the omelet without even asking. People's mouths drop open and it makes it all worth it right there.

It's really the food with you, more than the customers?

It is the food, it really is. It's the product. It's the fact that we're setting down in front of people the best food for this price anywhere in town, hands down. And I believe it. I love being on this side of it.

I want to go through and say, "Eat, eat, don't waste that food." I'm everybody's Jewish mother and I'm not even Jewish.

The quality aspect is still the best way to go?

Absolutely. It's the only way. If you cut corners, not only do you know it, but sooner or later everybody else will figure it out. It really is not worth it. It's much better to add whatever is necessary to the menu price . . . the nickel, or dime, or fifty cents needed to cover it. That's the way.

By the way, is this a partnership, or did you and Laurie incorporate?

Yes, we did. We are a corporation for tax reasons now, which is a new step for me. I've become one of the big kids. We incorporated one and a half months after we opened . . . Allen Ramey, Incorporated. Sounds pretty good!

What do you and Laurie see for the future? Any franchising?

No, we're not going to have any Blue Willow franchises, that's for sure. This is one of a kind. We are going to keep working hard with the Blue Willow . . . that's a large part of my future. There are some other things, though, that Tucson needs. It would be wonderful to be right in there on the ground floor, doing it. There are some other holes to fill up, besides omelets. We're looking in that direction.

In the next few years I think we'll be doing other business ventures together, my partner and I. Maybe a few other women we know who have things they would like to do . . . maybe they would like to do them all under *one* roof. The idea of the restaurant and poster gallery being so successful, we're pushing for the idea of maybe four or five businesses run by women . . . together.

*You two certainly could help others, especially those who
have never been in business and want to try.*

I wish anybody a lot of luck who goes into their own business. It's a hard
thing to do and there are people around that can help. There is the Retired
Businessmen's Association, which I really think a lot of . . . retired people
who have been in business themselves, who are willing to voluntarily sit
down and give you a rap on being in business for yourself.

I think it's hard because you have to be cut out for it. You should know
yourself. By the time you are mature, you should have a few clues as to your
personality defects and strengths.

If you're the kind of person who has a difficult time making decisions; are
not a good judge of character; can only do one thing at a time; get flustered
when things go wrong . . . don't do it. Work for somebody else until you
feel the confidence that you can take on almost any kind of stress without
completely messing up your head and personal life.

*You're obviously happy running your own business . . .
any regrets?*

None. I love it. I'm so spoiled that I simply couldn't work for anybody else
after working for myself this long. It gives you the challenge of having an
idea and actually following through and doing it. If it's successful, there's
nothing like it. If it's not successful, you just skip town . . . well, maybe,
you just start again . . . which is what I would have done if this hadn't
worked.

Success-Steps Analysis

At first glance, the Blue Willow venture seems somewhat of a departure
from the other interviews.

(a) There are numerous employees involved.

(b) The partners invested more initial capital than suggested by
our original guidelines.

Both factors, however, do not disqualify this example. The large number of employees, thirty, was partially necessitated by the unexpected volume of business and the resultant immediate success. The initial capital investment could have been considerably lessened by a bank loan, if the partners so desired.

Of greater importance, to those who wish an insight into the behind-the-scenes factors of a business start-up, are the lessons that can be absorbed from this venture. They include many of the entrepreneurial mandatories that are stressed by the consultants and authorities who are committed to the encouragement of small business.

It's worth reviewing a few of these "musts" as they pertain to the Blue Willow and its owners.

- The need for specific personality characteristics that enable one to cope with, and succeed in, their own business.

Both Janet Ramey and Laurie Allen measure up admirably in this area. Their attitude, drive, stamina, and very healthy outlook with relation to the Blue Willow are highly visible. Additionally, these characteristics are also evidenced by Laurie's other ongoing businesses and by Janet's previous ones.

- The desirability of examining one's skills, experience, and likes, in consideration of what type of business to start.

The choice of a restaurant was an easy one for Janet. All her experience pointed in that direction. But there was another, equally important factor involved. She thoroughly enjoyed the preparation of food, and liked seeing satisfied customers. At the same time, her partner's existing retail experience and graphics knowledge must have also been factored into their thinking and research toward the final determination of a combination-business selection.

- The prerequisite requirement of checking your market, the product fit, the competition, the location, et cetera.

Obviously, there was thought given to this mandatory consideration. A thorough survey of their marketplace resulted in flushing out specific areas of market needs that required fulfillment. Tucson could easily accomodate a restaurant that offered the specialty of a prolific variety of omelets and an accompanying selection of "health foods."

Although the Blue Willow's location on a street with fifteen other restaurants was not selected with that thought in mind, it seems to have become a distinct asset. In this heavily-traveled area, its existence was quickly noticed and within a short time the Blue Willow became a definite alternative to the many fast food, plasticized, franchise emporiums that lined the avenue.

- The need to establish and identify the differences between you and your competitors.

Here again, research and pre-planning paid off. Initial differences in the restaurant aspect were focused on . . . real, homemade food, a specialty of omelets, quality at reasonable prices, and some attractive health food menu items.

Added to that was the uniqueness of combining a poster gallery with the restaurant. The traffic pattern of going through the large, suitable-for-browsing, open area of the gallery to the restaurant, benefitted both business ventures. Since both were successful, the establishment of a positive identity and a competitive difference for the Blue Willow was assured.

- The advisability of professional help, especially in areas the beginner is not familiar with.

As Janet Ramey noted, "We had a lawyer, a real-estate agent, an accountant, and a lot of friends who've been very supportive. We had some people at the bank who knew us and that really helped." Note that even though both partners had some previous business experience, they were not averse to consulting with the professionals.

Although they had many problems with the bookkeeping for the first six months, they were well aware of its importance and did have a book-keeper from inception. The unexpected start-off volume and the book-keeper's nervous breakdown were the contributing factors to the initial records' being in shambles.

- The necessity of preparing a "business plan" before starting a venture.

Janet and Laurie did not start the Blue Willow Poster Gallery and Restaurant without planning. As a result, they knew what they wanted to do, where it would be done, and how to accomplish it. Their projections included concepts, renovations, start-up costs, product selections, personnel, salaries, and anticipated (though estimated roughly) annual volume. And, although changes are often necessary in initial plans, the target and direction were firmly established.

A review of these well-known mandatories is only the beginning when it comes to acquiring a knowledge and understanding of how new ventures start out. Somewhere in the background, there are a number of other less tangible factors, such as attitude, values, philosophy, and sensitivity. Janet Ramey expressed a number of thoughts in these areas:

". . . present a quality product and present it uniquely . . ."

". . . some ideas are great ideas, but they don't work and you have to accept a few of those, too . . ."

". . . you have to have a built-in work ethic unbelievably different from most people's . . ."

". . . you have to have the ability to put your own personal life aside for a while . . ."

". . . the person who owns the business is the one who sets the tone . . ."

". . . he's 68 years old and he's just the balance we need . . ."

". . . if you don't see the figures in black and white, you're just guessing . . ."

". . . your total source of income is what comes walking in the front door . . . that's all you have to work with . . ."

". . . as an owner, you never know what's going to happen . . . you have to be willing to get in there every day and hope it works out . . ."

". . . if you cut corners, not only do you know it, but sooner or later everybody else would figure it out . . ."

". . . being an owner is not a personality contest. It's hard to stay honest and direct and open with your employees . . . not too friendly, or too unfriendly . . ."

". . . our partnership has worked out beautifully because our friendship is the main event . . ."

". . . we're setting down in front of people the best food for this price anywhere in town . . . and I believe it . . . and I love being on this side of it . . ."

Provocative thoughts. Their essence is applicable to any venture the reader may be contemplating in the small-business arena.

The value of these interviews . . . in the entrepreneur's own words . . . is the inner-depth view they offer, where the why or how of making certain decisions becomes more apparent because of the thinking behind it all. This insight can stimulate your own thinking or, if the need exists, provoke you to expand your preliminary research into areas that were not completely explored.

Checking the Marketplace

Without question, starting a business of your own is a pretty serious undertaking. Nevertheless, that familiar scene of a cartoon face with a brightly lit bulb above the head is somewhat symbolic of how it all begins. For, above all, there *must* be an idea!

That idea may relate to a product or a service . . . and the end activity may concern its manufacture, its distribution, its sales, or its performance.

Super enthusiasm at this point is welcome, so long as it doesn't cloud the need for the many steps that must be taken to propel that idea into a business reality. One of the acknowledged mandatories is a preliminary research of the marketplace. This is where the well-known question-and-answer game of entrepreneurship takes on some form.

- How does your product or service fit into the present marketplace?

- Is there a market? Is there a need?

- Are there competitors?

- Why is your product or service better?

Admittedly, that's only the beginning of the questions. But, at the same time, getting to know the answers makes it easy to evaluate whether or not your idea can become an actual business. That's why you're urged to develop a "business plan" *before* you start.

Any kind of planning is a must! And, within the structure of that formal or informal business plan, one of the areas that does answer innumerable questions is the marketplace study. Even if you don't have the professional know-how to conduct and analyze a really extensive study, it's important to start out checking some of the basics. These are the initial facts you must have to determine your own first steps:

- **Identify your market.** This includes establishing that there is a need for your product or service. Will your product satisfy that need? What types of businesses will relate to your product? If consumers are involved, is there a specific age bracket, level of income, and/or definite locale to be targeted? Does the market depend on habit, customs, or seasons? Is the market segment large enough? Is there more than one market? Will the price of the product or service be a factor?

- **Assess competition.** Does it exist and where? What kind of competitors are they? What are their reputations? Is your product or service better? Comparable? More available? Less costly? Check out the differences and determine if they make your offering more marketable or less marketable.

- **Distribution.** What is the best way to reach your proposed markets? Retail selling or mail order? Through wholesalers and distributors? Or a combination of ways? Are purchase plans, consignment sales, franchises, or house parties the answer? Is the method of distribution dependent upon the nature of your advertising strategy or how the product is produced?

Is that all there is to it? Of course not. But a knowledge of these basic marketplace facts will surely facilitate an evaluation as to whether the idea can become a business. Without this knowledge, many a beginning enterprise has stumbled into oblivion . . . a type of casualty that can definitely be attributed to incompetency.

Because this initial information is so important in determining a go-ahead, some future entrepreneurs will consult a research agency or a local university with that kind of capability. But a great deal of this material is

available for you to dig out yourself. When it comes to consumer demographics . . . age, income brackets, population counts, and density . . .
it may be as close as the local chamber of commerce, the library, or your
state and city planning commissions. Additionally, this type of information
is often published by the banks and utility companies in an area and by
various federal agencies. Other places to check are the regional newspapers
and the specific trade association that relates to your business.

Hand in hand with that valuable information, and often because of it,
is the determination of your business location. Be it retail, manufacturing,
distribution, or service, the site location is an intrinsic part of the marketplace survey. The same sources of demographic material, just outlined,
can also be the information fountainheads to help you choose a successful
location.

- **Retail.** The choice of site will relate to the type of business, but
  many of the questions are the same. Is it close to transportation
  facilities? What about the income level of the surrounding population? Type of community? Proximity of competition? What are
  the benefits and drawbacks of a shopping-center location? A
  business district site? A suburban area? Does your business require a flow of people or will they seek you out? Must you be near
  your sources of supply? What size market or numbers of people
  are required to support your type of store? The neighboring stores
  . . . will they help draw the type customers you need? What
  about parking facilities? Do you require a loading and unloading zone in front of your shop? What are the rental and lease
  arrangements?

- **Manufacturing.** Will it be necessary to be close to suppliers? To
  customers? Do you require a plentiful supply of labor and available transportation? How will local taxes and regulations affect
  your operation? Are power costs within reason? Is a building
  necessary and shall you build, buy, or lease this facility? Does
  your building site comply with the necessary permits, zoning,
  and environmental regulations? Will you subcontract to other
  manufacturers or will you simply assembly the product? Do you
  require ample parking, shipping, and receiving areas? If you start
  out in a small factory space, will there be room for expansion? Can
  you combine office and manufacturing areas in the selected site?

- **Services.** Can you start your repair or maintenance service business at home, in the garage, or in a small office? Does the business require a prime location for "drop-in" trade . . . watch repair, shoe repair, et cetera? If so, many of the retail store questions will also apply. Is it the type business that isn't dependent upon high traffic . . . carpentry, electrical, plumbing, et al? If so, the premises should have adequate parking, loading space, easy access to the street, and not be too difficult to find. Will you concentrate on businesses, residences, or individuals? Will this affect the choice of location site?

Here again, resolving these questions should supply you with enough information to intelligently plan your steps, especially the initial ones. Of course, depending upon the business you select, there will be many additional questions that will have to be added to the above. In the event you buy an existing business, this same research should be conducted, along with all the other factors that have to be evaluated in any buy/sell situation.

Don't think that checking the marketplace is the end-all of your acquisition of preliminary business knowledge. There are many other areas that you will be forced to become familiar with. One example is the very allied field of marketing and advertising . . . which affects all business, both large and small.

Marketing encompasses all functions and activities necessary to get the product or service from producer to user. Your local library and the various trade associations will have a great deal of material in this area.

Read . . . ask questions . . . interview others in the same business . . . and, above all, plan your actions.

Keep in mind that your business direction will be a two-fold one. To satisfy the user's needs and desires . . . and to satisfy your company's objectives—profit, growth, survival.

7　Becoming a Retailer

Genie Lehr, 49, had never been in a retail business before and when she purchased this one, it was a completely new learning experience.

Her awareness of this lack of retail knowledge is what led to the final decision to buy a store, rather than start one from scratch. But, here again, there was no guarantee of success and no assurance that things would be easy.

After one year of operation, she has gained a good deal of experience and confidence. She admits it's only a beginning and looks forward to additional study and growth.

THE CHEESE GENIE *
HASTINGS-ON-HUDSON,
NEW YORK

Hastings is a small suburban village of approximately 9,000 people. The store had been in operation for three years before Genie Lehr purchased it in the spring two years ago.

Her first change involved the use of her own name . . . from the previous owner's, The Mad Cheese, to the present name, The Cheese Genie.

I know you have never really been in business before.
Why now, at this stage of life? Is it just a hobby?

Absolutely not! My three children are grown, in their twenties, but it wasn't a question of time hanging heavy or the need for something to do.

When they were in high school, I was a professional fund raiser for five years. Then I went back to college for a while to get my degree in behavioral science, with the thought of returning to fund raising. But no one really wanted to pay for this service, so I started to look around for a business that might bring in a reasonable income.

What were the first steps . . . how did you start looking around?

I did a lot of reading. In fact, I even read your first book during my research. I also spoke to friends who were or had been in business. Then I went to the local area's Small Business Administration office to get advice. They talked to me and gave me a number of booklets to read and further my research.

Was the SBA helpful? I've heard many good reports, but there are others who were disappointed.

Yes, I think they can help. In my case, though, they were fairly discouraging about my reasons for going into business. They viewed mine as a second-income business, it wasn't one of survival. At the same time, my lack of experience . . . never having been in business or mastered a special skill . . . I guess this bothered them a bit, too.

While you continued your research, did you go to a business broker to see what was available? Were you firm on buying rather than starting?

No, I just looked in the papers . . . casually checked out the ads. I guess it wasn't a question of "let's find something, quick." At that stage it wasn't an urgent or immediate thing. The business broker idea didn't enter my mind. I thought the direct ads themselves would show more variety.

As far as buying . . . well, I thought there would be less risk involved because you could *see* more of everything. You would have an idea of the sales, the customers, the expenses . . . all the kinds of things you couldn't be sure of if you were starting a new situation. My husband was formerly in accounting and this would be very helpful when it came to checking out an established venture.

In fact, he ran across an available business, but it was located in New York City and required seven days a week. That wasn't the kind of time that appealed to me, since I am very involved as a regional vice president in a volunteer organization.

Was the cheese shop one of many retail units that you looked at?

No. Stangely enough, it was the first business that I looked at, because the food aspect did interest me. I had no previous experience in it, but our whole family enjoys gourmet food. My two daughters are vegetarians, so we had a lot of experience with cheeses and dairy foods. I guess you can say that most of my knowledge in this field comes from being a consumer.

I saw the ad in *The New York Times*—it was not advertised in the local papers—and I recognized the phone number. The store was in the village adjoining my home. It was somewhat familiar to me because I had shopped there on a few occasions.

Since it was close to me, there would be no commuting involved and, additionally, it could be a five-day work week. He had been open a few hours on Sunday, but that could be discontinued. So there were many positives involved. I visited the store a few times and then we started to discuss a possible purchase.

By the way, why did he want to sell? What were the details?

Originally he said for health reasons . . . that's something you can always be apprehensive about. And, as it turned out, he left for Florida to start a new venture.

His initial asking price was approximately $29,000. This included furniture and fixtures, the stock, good will, and the present lease. There's no question that it's a small store, about 12 feet by 24 feet, and another 12 by 12 feet that is our storeroom and utilities area. Still in all, there's plenty of equipment.

In the back we have shelving, a side-by-side home refrigerator/freezer, hot water tank, gas heater, sink, et cetera. The store area proper contains a high double glass door commercial refrigerator, a low showcase refrigerator with work counter above, a coffee grinder, digital scale, knives, chopping block, adding machine, and shelving.

The lease had only a short term to run, but a renegotiation with the landlord proved to be no trouble at all, very pleasant, in fact. He was more than fair.

When your husband checked the figures, how did they come out? Were there any difficulties?

It was a fairly modest operation. Gross sales the year before were somewhere around $63,000 with a net return of 9 or $10,000. His most recent gross was approaching $71,000 with a corresponding increase in returns. Since it was after the holidays, the inventory was down. Knowing he was selling the business, the owner felt no urgency to restock.

Interestingly enough, my husband was able to look over the books and records without putting up a binder . . . "earnest money," I think they call it. There was no difficulty there; the young owner was quite cooperative.

Although the store was small, the potential convinced us to negotiate a purchase. There were a number of favorable factors, especially for someone new to running a business:

> proximity to our home
> compactness of the store
> a clean, non-strenuous operation
> an inventory of consumable, repeat items
> a village clientele and atmosphere
> some knowledge of the product (as a consumer)

My husband had explained that a similar store in a metropolitan area would make much more money, but I felt that this might be just right for my first business experience. And, I guess by that time, I was mentally sprucing up that little shop, making it look better, with even more potential.

How did you resolve the final details . . . the financing, the contract, and so on?

My husband and our lawyer worked with the young man and his lawyer. The purchase price was all cash, about $25,000. By contract, the owner would stay with me for two weeks to help in the transition. About 25 percent of the cash was put into escrow for 90 days. That turned out to be a very, very good thing!

It seemed money was owed to a number of suppliers and there were also a number of liens in existence. In addition, some taxes were still outstanding. Without the escrow, it would have been disastrous! I see now how people can get trapped, if they are novices and don't have professional help. Incidentally, that owner didn't stay the full two weeks. I think it bothered him to see sales going on that weren't part of his income, and he really was anxious to leave town to start his next venture.

What did you do to improve the store, yourself, your expertise?

The first major visible change was to clean the store. Then I studied the stock, did a lot of tasting so as to understand the flavor differences and make personal recommendations to the customers. I did a lot more reading in areas that would be helpful. The Sunday hours were cut out and there's now a 10 AM to 6 PM, Tuesday through Saturday schedule.

My daughter helped tremendously in those first months. Although my husband takes care of the books, I am now much more familiar with that area. As time went on, I doubled the original stock and started to weed out many items that were on the shelves with no movement. In a sense, studying the stock also helped teach me what not to do.

Frankly, the first three months or so, I was very apprehensive and nervous. Now, after a full year, it's a great deal better. I have much more confidence and experience.

It sounds as if you have been working off the previous owner's negatives. Would you cover that facet a little further?

Well, you're right. For example I did announce the new ownership with window posters and local advertising. But I was told that people recognized that fact almost immediately, simply from the improved cleanliness of the shop.

He had stocked some health-food items, deliberately I think, to compete with a well-established and fine health-food store around the corner. I made a point to eliminate a number of those lines . . . the flours, all grain products, legumes . . . things customers can get much fresher, because of the faster turnover, in that store. At the same time it was important to create and establish my own shop's unique gourmet identity in the community.

There was an overstock of boxed chocolates, which do not have a long shelf life. I discovered this spoilage factor fairly quickly—and yet the previous owner had been there three years. Some customers who returned because of the new ownership commented that their recent lack of patronage had been a result of occasionally receiving spoiled merchandise.

Being close to New York is an asset for fast contact with our suppliers so there really is no need to overstock and encourage spoilage. Our variety of coffee beans is greater than the previous owner's stock and they aren't just lying in sacks on the floor. We put in some plastic viewing bins and intend to put in more . . . it's cleaner and more attractive for impulse buying.

Have your suppliers been helpful?

Yes, very helpful. I didn't realize how much until much further on in my ownership. Anytime I asked any kind of question, they were ready to help. Also they would discuss and advise as to what type of items would sell best during specific times of the year.

I recently hired someone for the day and attended a coffee seminar given by one of the coffee companies. Even though I have several books on coffee, it enhanced my knowledge. What I learned about merchandising the product was invaluable.

What about growth? That's going to be difficult in this small space.

Well, I'm putting more money into coffee rather than shelf goods because it is a faster turnover item . . . consumed quicker, like the cheeses. The display has been changed, so that people are more aware of the coffee choices. There's an electric coffee maker in the corner . . . visible through the main window . . . to induce people to taste the various blends. That's where I expect to get some growth.

Additionally, our gourmet foods are more varied. The static items are just about cleaned off through specials and markdowns. And, because I had to learn how to buy, there are better offerings for the shopper who relates to the gourmet foods. As a long-time consumer, I'm familiar with the items that are considered popular in this field. This can mean growth, too.

Soon I'll be changing the store around. That's where the first year's money will go.

This is the end of your first year. Did the gross sales measure up to the seller's statement? Is the store profitable?

Not quite. But I can see the improvement for the future. He did have a good German clientele because he spoke German fluently. We have lost some of them and kept others. Many people who did not shop because they had no rapport with him are finally coming in. Some of them, after a year, are finally realizing that it's a completely new deal now.

Even in this initial stage, though, I think it's profitable. I'm taking a salary and the shelves have been doubled in inventory . . . that's where the profit has gone. Next year we may even get a bonus!

How do you personally feel after this first year? Glad you went ahead?

Oh, I still very much enjoy what I'm doing. There are times, of course, when I'd like to get out in the middle of the day and walk in the beautiful sunshine. With a one-person store, you are tied down . . . even vacations will be difficult, although the store can be closed down for a specific time.

There's a certain amount of creativity in the store that I'm enthused about. Making up gift baskets, particularly around Christmas- and Easter-time, is very satisfying. I enjoy putting together different combinations of gourmet foods and cheeses, basket suggestions, and displays.

And then there are the window displays. I change them about every three weeks and people do stop and look. It's important for them to relate to the many things we have to offer . . . and not think of us as a grocery store. The Cheese Genie is something special.

Also, there's accomplishment. For a person who hasn't been in business before, I've done it, and that means a lot. Knowing that my personality and perseverance have succeeded and been accepted by others is pretty satisfying.

You have no hired help. Is it just the family that chips in?

Yes. My son does so once in a while. I'm here five days a week and my husband helps out on Saturdays. In the busy season, my daughter will also devote some time.

It's a full-time job but I also do a number of other things. Monday is my day in New York with the volunteer organization, for example. Perhaps at some later date I'll be able to make use of part-time help. Basically, though, it's a business that can be handled, specifically because it is a five-day week with no late evenings.

Are there any permits, regulations, or licenses involved in this kind of food shop?

There's the sales tax, of course. The Health Department checks the premises every two months to see if everything is up to their standards. This survey relates to anyone selling food and packaged foods. There's a different code if you are serving foods.

I learned from the Weights and Measures people when they came to inspect the scale that every item must be priced marked. It should also be marked on the shelves in front of the items. That's something I wanted for myself anyway for my own information.

The previous owner had nothing marked, everything was in his head. If you look in the glass-door refrigerator, you'll notice that all the cheese portions are each labeled with the name and price per weight unit. I think it's a good selling practice; the customer can see each of the cheeses that are being suggested and it's a nice display.

You've told me about a number of your positive moves. Were there any mistakes along the way?

Not really, no mistakes. We did have to put in air conditioning . . . it didn't exist. We also found it necessary to redo the electrical wiring as a safety measure.

I've discovered that advertising is really my most shaky area. I'm not sure that any of the advertising I did was worthwhile at all. I have no idea of what I'm doing in this area and no idea as to how to approach it. The former owner said, "Oh, you don't have to advertise at all, they'll just come in off the street." I'm afraid that's not quite it, either.

I have ads in the weekly local paper and have indulged in some promotional events. This is our first anniversary month and with every purchase of a pound of coffee, we give a quarter pound of another blend free. We do get a certain following that comes back, all the time, but I'm looking to build a business and not stay at one level.

Naturally, there's competition. The supermarket and a goodly number of delicatessens are in the village proper. Although they don't stock a complete line of gourmet foods and cheeses, they do have a number of items. Join that with the fact that people like to do one-shop shopping and getting them here does become a problem.

I've neglected my homework in the area of advertising and I guess the library and those government booklets had better be my next step.

> *Genie, right now you're building up a good deal of positive word-of-mouth advertising. The shop is obviously a much better one than it was. Our interview has been interrupted by a number of customers and I must say, I've been impressed by the way you handle them. You answer their inquiries intelligently, make suggestions, have them taste the various cheeses, explain the differences and the locale of origin, offer items that will complement them, and physically wrap up the total sale. In other words, your experience is showing!*

Success-Steps Analysis

Awareness can often be like a beacon of light that cuts through the murky darkness of the unknown. When a person who has never been in business before decides to make the entrepreneurial move, you can be sure there are plenty of shadowy paths ahead.

Fortunately, Genie Lehr was aware of her limitations and the risks involved . . . that was a definite plus! And she took action in a number of ways, in an effort to help make the odds come up in her favor:

> a great deal of reading about small businesses
> talking with others who were in small business
> getting some advice from SBA
> deciding to buy rather than start fresh
> obtaining accounting help from her husband
> involving the family when needed

As in all cases, the aspect of pre-planning is still the mandatory preliminary to actually start out. Knowing her lack of experience could be a costly drawback, the decision to buy a business made the owner/manager plunge somewhat less risky. That in turn helped considerably in an area that most people don't think about . . . her beginning attitude. She admitted to being nervous about the venture, but she also felt some confidence about being successful because of the way she would be starting.

With no past history of entrepreneurship, all the everyday routines of retailing would present formidable obstacles, especially if a tremendous amount of preparation had not taken place. Genie, by buying an established business, also bought time . . . time to learn on-the-job with actualities instead of print/hearsay.

Although she selected the first business she investigated, don't forget it was the first ad that interested her. Gourmet foods was not a hobby, but something definitely familiar to both Genie and her family. That kind of thinking, premeditated or accidental, is part and parcel of the "what type of business should I go into" evaluation. Her knowledge of that field, even as a consumer, was something tangible to bring to the unknown retail field she was about to enter.

Obviously, there was an existing pattern to the present store and by initially following it, the start-off was facilitated for Genie. Her concentration could then be applied to the immediate needs of her customers and her own need to develop retail skills. For the moment, she didn't have to be frustrated about type of inventory, gross sales, expenses, suppliers, insurance, equipment, et cetera. They were already there!

The beauty of all that is, it's much easier to review and analyze something that exists rather than something still to be structured. That's exactly what Genie Lehr did as she learned what the business was all about. She experimented with the stock by adding many new items; deleting slow-moving and competitive ones; stressing more coffee sales; cutting down on spoilage factors; and by sampling cheeses and coffee blends so as to better advise the customers.

Although it isn't a twelve-hour-a-day type of business, she is devoting full-time to the business all the necessary hours. Her commitment also relates to continuing her reading and research plus the promise to find out a lot more about the advertising problem. But, even there, all is not lost.

Remember some of her improvements . . . every cheese with a name tag; plastic bins for coffee-bean exposure; the coffee pot is on, try it; three-week window display changes; emphasis on a unique identity. I hope Genie realizes that all these positive steps are the second cousin to advertising and she's certainly moving in the right direction.

It's only been one year of actual operation and this review of success steps has to be limited because it's only a beginning. Even in that short space of time, however, the familiar steps of successful entrepreneurship are there . . . capitalization, risk, commitment, awareness, pro-and-con analysis, planning, follow-through, and perseverance. The relevant skills and experience of small-business ownership were a couple of the missing ingredients in her background, but the operation of The Cheese Genie this past year has gone a long way toward supplying them on an actuality basis.

At the same time, Genie Lehr is looking forward to future growth. She will soon be changing the store around. No doubt the confidence gained from a full year of retail management will stand her in good stead when she incorporates her ideas into a new look. It will be one more step in making it her store, her own business.

Buying a Business

There are a number of ways to get started in a small business of your own. The one thing they all have in common, however, is the necessity to do your homework by pre-planning. To some would-be entrepreneurs, buying an existing business seems to indicate that because everything is already set up and going, there's less need for heavy research and planning.

Not so! Perhaps the purchase of a business does call for a different emphasis from starting from ground zero, but planning is still a vital step. In fact, the Small Business Administration's approach is that the same factors you plan for in starting a business apply equally well to buying one . . . plus there is an increased need to check out a number of additional points.

- **Personality characteristics.** Whether you start or buy, it's important to have the health, drive, skills, and commitment that are necessary for owner/managership.

- **Choosing the type business.** In purchasing an existing venture, this fact is still dependent upon your experience, skills, hobbies, or basic interests. This evaluation applies in all types of small-business start-ups.

- **Capitalization.** In starting, it's important to project what monies you will need to get going. In buying, this factor will determine the size and perhaps the type of business that you will be able to consider. In either case, the sources of capital must be determined and activated.

- **Form of business.** Many small businesses are sole proprietorships, but partnerships and corporations are also chosen. Here again, that decision must still be made in any of the ways you choose to become an entrepreneur.

- **Location.** An essential ingredient in all forms and types of business, whether you buy, franchise, start from scratch, or begin part-time. Buying does not relieve you from researching whether the location is desirable or just so-so.

- **Business Plan.** Even a simplified one is mandatory. Admittedly, purchasing an established business will supply you with many of these factors, but future projections, growth, and competition must still be evaluated and planned for.

As listed above, it's obvious that the SBA's contention seems to be very valid. To that list, then, we must add those *additional* areas that should be analyzed when buying a business:

- **Locating opportunities.** If you know the type of business you want to buy, then the trade sources of that industry are a good potential. This would include the trade publications, manufacturers, distributors, suppliers, and the trade association.

Newspapers ads are an excellent source. Be sure to peruse all the papers in the area that is under your consideration. Often a seller will not use the local paper if he does not wish those around him to know about the sale.

Business brokers or realtors who handle commercial sales can be very helpful. In one office there may be a variety of offerings. A surface perusal and discussion of the offerings as a group may give you a better insight into the idea of gross sales versus returns, asking price versus gross sales, down payments versus sales price, et cetera. Although the brokers get their commission from the sellers, if they are reputable in their field, it is to their own interests that you succeed. Otherwise, potential future business ties to each are down the drain. The reliable broker looks to match the buyer and seller, so that both come out well and the possibility of litigation is non-existant.

- **Reason for sale.** Don't accept what's offered as gospel. It's like the used car that was only driven by "a little old lady every once in a while." Ill health is often given as the reason and it may not be anything like that. Retirement is another one, along with "I have other business interests."

There may be truth there, but it will be your job to check out the other possibilities that may be the real reason. Competition may be too heavy; the marketing area may be changing toward the negative; there's a short lease; manufacturing facilities are not up to snuff; the products are outdated; cash flow may be a problem because of the type of accounts receivables.

The main caution here is to do your homework and investigate. If you're looking at an operation going downhill, you must be thoroughly experienced in that business and be a whiz at evaluating the problems and possible profit potential. Otherwise, forget it!

- **Checking the business.** At this point you're going for the "brass ring." To determine a reasonable purchase price, you must evaluate the past, present, and future earnings. Records must be analyzed and you should have professional assistance.

An accountant who knows something about that specific type of business would be ideal. He or she can review current records of sales and operating ratios, as well as dig back a few years to review the owner's past income. Federal and state tax returns will also be necessary at this point. A projection of sales, expenses, cash flow, and profits should be made for the next year.

There may be an "on" and "off the books" structure, which requires extensive probing in order to verify accuracy. Not to be neglected are those who have relevant information, the banker, landlord, neighboring businesses, suppliers, and insurance broker.

If the seller is reluctant to supply the necessary information, that may be a problem in going ahead at all. Without thorough information and investigation, the buyer will be at a terrible disadvantage in trying to determine the value and profit potential of the business.

Besides records of sales, expenses, and returns, there are numerous other areas that must be evaluated. That's why buying a business is not as simple as it sounds. What about the need to check . . .

> inventory
> furniture and fixtures
> equipment
> present lease
> good will
> suppliers
> personnel
> customer contacts, lists
> accounts receivables
> liens, back taxes
> permits, licenses

There may be more, but that's enough to start you thinking about the total picture. When you actually start to finalize the purchase, get a reliable lawyer! A sales contract should have a professional by your side. The sales price is something you have to negotiate based upon your accountant's reports and the businesses' profit potential. After taking into consideration all the furniture and fixtures, equipment, inventory, and good will, the major factor is still future profits as a return on your investment.

Don't forget an escrow fund to make sure that all conditions of the sale have been met before final title and distribution of funds. If the seller is taking part cash and part notes, he may be also willing to stay with the new owner for a short transition period. The "notes" structure could be a definite asset for it's incentive on the seller's part to root for your success. A transition period may give the new owner a smooth introduction from the seller to customers, suppliers, and existing personnel, if any. It also facilitates an understanding of present operational patterns.

Keep in mind that it's foolish to rush into a purchase of a business without adequate preparation. You have much to lose . . . perhaps your life savings. Remember, the pitfalls are for the buyer, not the seller!

8 What About Mail Order?

There's that old cliché, "Life begins at 40."

Very often it does become a truism, in the sense that another aspect of life begins at that age. Sometimes with great forethought; occasionally from a series of unstructured events that merged together.

Hugh Fordin, at 40, didn't know it then, but that's how it all started.

A hobby he dabbled in became a small business and now, with spectacular growth, it takes up all of his time, energy, and enthusiasm.

Although this is his first crack at being the owner/operator of a small business, Fordin enjoys the challenge and from now on that's where he wants to stay.

D R G RECORDS, INC. *
NEW YORK, N.Y.

Hugh Fordin has been a record lover since childhood, then a film and theater buff. Somewhere along the line he spent time with a production unit of 20th Century Fox and put in about three years as head of casting for Broadway producer David Merrick.

He continued his interest in the entertainment field by devoting a good deal of time and research to writing a successful book about the many great MGM musical films produced by Arthur Freed. *The World of Entertainment* was reviewed by one critic who said, "I count it among the ten most valuable film books I've read."

The research for the book sparked the record idea . . .
what were the actualities of that?

Writing the book I noted the interesting fact that many songs were taped for particular movies but never showed up in the final film. Either they were cut out or the star couldn't appear as originally scheduled.

Some examples were Judy Garland and "I'll Plant My Own Tree"; Fred Astaire and "Got a Brand New Suit." For *On a Clear Day* there was Barbra Streisand's "Wait 'Til You're 65," which was never in the finished film.

I asked MGM for permission to use the master tapes to make a small number of records . . . 1,000 copies. More for a hobby, sort of a side-line venture that didn't require much time. They gave me the rights and that was the beginning of my record education.

Since I didn't know anything about records, I went to a jobbing contractor, a servicing outlet. You just deliver a master tape and the art work. In thirty days or so, they deliver 1,000 records for *x* number of dollars.

How were the records going to be handled? Did you have any plans? Were you set up at all?

Well, I wanted to work on writing a second book, so I set up a little mail-order operation out of a friend's apartment. He was an actor out of work. I was going to put a few classified ads in *High Fidelity* magazine and the *Village Voice* paper.

I told him, "Look, it's no big deal and you can follow up on it while you have the spare time. The money will be coming in to a P.O. box. You just go there every *few* days . . . not every day. When you get the orders, deposit the checks and wait about two weeks. Then send them the records."

Oh, yes, before I even started, even though it was just a sideline, I remembered to get a business certificate and open a bank account. My regular lawyer suggested an accountant who would come in every quarter and do the taxes and all that sort of stuff. That knowledge came from a previous hobby-investment I had in an antique shop with a friend.

That first record was called *Cut* and Out Take Records was the company name. At that time I sent Rex Reed a copy because he had really liked my book on MGM musicals. Unbeknownst to me, he devoted an entire Sunday column across the country to the record. He noted that I had only pressed 1,000 copies and those who were interested had better get their money in.

Mainly because of that we were swamped with *8,000 orders!*

How did you handle that first inventory crisis?

That was only the half of it! It was the summer and the record contractor's staff was on vacation. I didn't know where in God's name I was going to get those other records. Luckily, the secretary was there and she explained how it all gets done. First the sleeves are printed and they're glued on to board; then from the fabricator it goes to the pressing plant and once there, they'll press the records. Don't forget, this series of steps wasn't for a new start-up situation, it was for an existing product.

So I went ahead and got each step going myself, billing the contractor of course, because I didn't know what they were normally charged for anything like that. Fortunately it was successful, and many people wrote in and said "What about Volume 2?" For no specific reason, I had put Volume 1 on the cover of that first record.

When I asked the contractor about better sound for the next record, he said I would have to go into the studio and sit down with the man who cuts the lacquer. "What's the lacquer?" You cut a lacquer first before you get the metal stamper. "What's a metal stamper?" That's what you make the records from. Of course, there were other steps in between, but that's how initial education goes . . . how you get to know more and more about your business. Anyway, we did produce Volume 2 and by that time I was also selling to a few stores.

Since it was mostly mail order, how did you tackle the follow-up mailings?

Oh, there's an interesting anecdote to that . . . luck, pure luck. Channel 13 of PBS has an auction every year to raise funds. A month before I started Out Take Records, their auction offered $500 worth of computer time. I figured it might be good to use for my book research, so I bid $25. When nobody else offered more, it was mine.

Later on, when all of those 8,000 orders came in, I had the names and addresses put on the computer. To this day everything I do with my mailers is through the computer . . . so are my financial records, P and L figures, and percentages. I'm sold on that!

That computer setup helped a lot with inquiries and sales for volumes 2 and 3. I stopped at Volume 3 because the AFM (American Federation of

Musicians) wanted payments of $9 per musician per track, payable to the union's retirement fund. These songs were never recorded for records, just films, but that's what stopped those releases of Out Take Records cold. The extra costs would have resulted in a total loss.

What was the thinking then? Did the idea of a hobby change to a business?

No, not yet. While I was still going with Out Takes and visiting a few stores, the next idea developed. Up in the Doubleday's buyer's office I noticed an old album of Nancy Walker and Elaine Stritch and I asked, "Why don't you reissue these? Nancy Walker's a big TV name now, maybe it would work for you." Well, their Dolphin label was no longer active and they didn't have any facilities, so I asked them to sell or license the old Dolphin masters to me. They agreed.

This is where my record lawyer handled the licensing agreement and I added some more knowledge to my record education. I then realized that there must be a lot of albums around that were not available anymore, which people would want in their collections.

One of my own old favorites was *Funny Face,* the Audrey Hepburn–Fred Astaire film musical. My record lawyer suggested a letter to those who owned it with a proposal for a licensing agreement. Sure enough, six weeks later we concluded a licensing deal.

We still worked out of the original apartment, but we were getting bigger, so I took my first step and rented a basement. There we were doing the shipping and stocking all the records. By this time we had volumes 1, 2, and 3 of the outtakes from the MGM musicals, as well as Nancy Walker, Elaine Stritch, and *Funny Face.* And I was still writing and researching the second book.

Those licensing agreements sound very legal; were you still in a very casual overall operation?

Somewhat. But now it started to get more structured. We became a corporation because I didn't want to be personally liable and we were getting larger. My regular lawyer set up the corporation and the record lawyer handled all the licensing and record deals.

Incidentally, let's bring up the accountant again. If you're in a specialized business, get an accountant who knows *that* particular business! It's the biggest mistake I made. It's not only the books for tax purposes and everything else, but when I wanted to know how much royalty we paid Nancy Walker or Elaine Stritch, he couldn't tell me. All the costs were jumbled together, that kind of thing. He had set it up like a hobby, not a business. It's vital to allocate costs and charges for each album or special situation. If the initial books are set up for these specifics, there's no problem along the way.

Even though I had been treating this as a sideline, an accountant familiar with the record field would have set it up the correct way. It was still a small operation . . . the volume of business wasn't 8,000 copies on every record, more like 2,000–2,500. Walker and Stritch weren't big sellers, although I didn't lose money on them. *Funny Face,* yes, was a good seller but it came out at a bad time of the year. Then, I didn't know what time of year was good, bad, or better. I hadn't been in the business long enough. But you keep learning . . . on the job!

It was all a matter of absorption. I was trying to understand everything about the record business, the licensing deals, royalties, and marketing. I couldn't go to school and have someone teach me about marketing a record because there's no such thing. Anyway—it's damn hard to predict success in the entertainment field!

I followed my natural instincts because I've been a lover of recorded sound since I was a kid. Years ago I had a collection of 10,000 records. My tax accountant said, "You're crazy, you don't play them all. Why don't you give them to a university and get a tax deduction?" So I gave up 2,000 records and now—who knew I'd be *selling* records?—I'm buying some of that very same stuff back to get the original art for the record jackets.

When you license material, they usually don't have the original art. Part of my marketing concept with the oldies is to recreate the album as it was originally done . . . great performances, nostalgia, the complete feeling.

It's obvious you were headed for a total commitment to a small business. When did it come about and why do you think it happened?

Yes, I guess it was working up to that all along. Without investing much money, I found myself tieing up a lot of products for reissue . . . not trying to get it all, just things that I really wanted and liked. Unconsciously, it seems, I knew that some day I was going to make this a business. I didn't want someone else to get the same idea.

I've always worked for other people, but I'd get frustrated after awhile because I would try to help them as if it were my own business. But they don't really want that help. Stay in your slot! Don't tell them how to save! Spend money for them, that's okay!

And, in other areas, things change and the bloom gets off the rose. When I was writing, it was a personal challenge . . . most all of it was under my own control. Now I think that starting a business is the most exciting thing in the world. Every day when I wake up, it's another challenge, another bit of excitement.

About a year after this all started, one of the old albums I was thinking of reissuing featured Comden and Green. Since they were on Broadway, I called them and asked about doing an album of their present *live* performance rather than redoing the old one. They agreed and I got my first taste of producing an album . . . of sitting and making judgments.

Wasn't that costly in relation to your usual reissue royalties?

Yes, but not that costly because I made private participation arrangements with them. They were eager to have an album done, so certain costs were not prohibitive. And they knew that I was a really interested partner.

That's also pretty much part of the concept for my business, of being *that* concerned for both the records and the artists. There are a number of artists who don't want to go to major companies any more. They've been there before and they see that if a record comes out and doesn't do anything, it's deleted and put into the hopper. It's not a question of hand-holding the artists, but they would like to see somebody there helping them, seeing what's going on, guiding the situation.

Going back to your original question, when I did the Comden and Green album, I was feeling my druthers and took these offices. That's when I started to really concern myself about a business, hiring a secretary, doing mail order the proper way, putting everything on the computer, and so on. Scared? Yes, I was. I even got someone else to take part of the office space and split the rent. Now it was a total commitment . . . the real move. One does get apprehensive at that stage of things. But the second book, *A Biography of Oscar Hammerstein II,* was finished, and I was ready to devote a lot more time to the business.

What would you say your initial investment totaled, and does that include salary?

Initially, ten thousand dollars. I haven't put any more money into it. Of course, there were times when it was tight . . . *very tight.* But no sheriff at the door and no lawsuits. [knocks wood.]

As far as salary, there was none the first year. I started taking salary the second year, and it killed me, taking it! Really, I felt that I was robbing somebody. But, of course, that's a familiar story for the small, beginning entrepreneur.

Now it's been almost three years. I'm living very comfortably. There are three employees with me and next week we're moving up to a larger space, three times the size of this one. It's not the glamour, it's not for show, it's because I'm expanding. We need the space and now I can afford it. Funny thing, when my co-tenant moved out, I wondered how I was going to pay the extra $150 a month. Now I'm going up to $1,000!

The movie outtakes was short-lived. How did your mail order proceed from there?

The mail order has grown. Of the original list of 8,000, about half remained. That was to be expected, because the first records were specialty items. Since then, however, we have built up to 12,000 fairly faithful supporters.

I don't believe in classified ads, because although you may sell one particular record, you aren't generally going to get constant business. What I have done, which has proven very effective, is to insert a questionnaire card in every record. It asks if the purchaser wishes to be put on our mailing list and receive a catalog. We even get some demographics . . . what business they're in, where they bought the record, what type they like, et cetera. It also helps my evaluation too, because they're not afraid to take me apart or commend me. And, if they have a defective record, we write them back and say send it back to us, if not the store.

The return questionnaire works and it doesn't cost the buyer anything; we pay the return postage. All in all, those cards have added 5,000 buying names to our lists.

We've tried lists, rented lists, but they haven't paid off for us because we're in a special market and maybe our customers aren't on lists. But we're not abandoning that avenue. We'll try again somewhere, perhaps by testing an active list of RCA, Columbia House, or another record club. It's not a hopeless situation. You just have to get the right list.

So, here again, this marketing and advertising aspect was something you had to absorb via trial and error.

Absolutely. For example, we had a one-man mail-order office in England. Well, EMI, who are importers and sell to the record stores, did such a fantastic job over there, that it killed our mail-order business. People in England aren't as far from a record store as people are here . . . it's a much smaller country. So they were close enough to shop in the store and we had to phase the office out.

The same thing with record sales. When our second mailing went out, we were not giving a discount. We hadn't given one on the first mailing. Then we found the orders starting to weaken. It weakened because many people were able to get to a discount store and order the record for less, and they were willing to wait for delivery. They also saved on our postage charges.

So I started to compete pricewise with the discount stores. Then I included an incentive. When I'd come out with six new albums, if a mail-order buyer bought all six, I'd give one of the older albums free! This, incidentally, was disastrous to those outfits who bought our records and had their own mail-order setup. They said they couldn't compete with me because of my prices and the free incentive albums. That was unfortunate, because I really wasn't trying to kill their business, I just wanted to keep and build up my own mail order.

One great marketing aspect we have in the record business is the reviews of our records by columnists across the country. Most of them have been extremely favorable and they're read by people who are interested in recorded sound, the potential buyers. I also do reprints of them and insert them into my catalog folio. It's a form of PR that's hard to beat.

What about fulfillment? How do you do your shipping?

We've always handled it ourselves. I haven't gone to a fulfillment house and doubt that I ever will. Initially we shipped fourth class because most mail buyers are accustomed to the allowance of four to six weeks for delivery. But we changed that after adding things up. There's waiting on line at the post office . . . record shipments that don't get there . . . occasional records that *do* get there, but in halves . . . and even some people trying to pull a fast one, saying they never got their order.

Now everything is UPS. That's part of the special service I give my mail-order customers. It's much faster, I have a signature, and insurance, and our costs are pretty much in a break-even situation. We charge $1.25 for postage and handling . . . it's only ninety cents locally and about $1.40 to California, so it averages out.

We ship immediately upon receipt of the order. Both of my accountants, the one I fired and my present record accountant, have asked me how long I hold the checks before shipping. When I said I don't, they both groaned. But, let's see . . . in three years of mail-order operation we've only had six checks bounce and I think three of those made good. That's it. We don't wait anymore.

Hugh, what can you tell someone who wants to start mail order . . . what about product, price, costs, and so on?

Well, product is important. That's going to be up to them, but it still relates to finding something that's needed or wanted and is not easily available. Maybe I was fortunate in that my kind of company didn't exist at all. In fact, after the second year people started to say to me, "How come nobody ever thought of this before?"

When it comes to records, most people and companies think in terms of hundreds of thousands and more. But there's enough markup to be able to work within the limited-edition aspect, if you keep your operation in comparative terms. The reissue or re-release idea was a different way to go and it related to my own love of recorded sound as a collector. The material I'm using was already recorded and my licensing agreements take care of the royalty percentages involved. Perhaps this kind of thinking can also work in other industries and situations.

Before you start your mail-order campaign or spend the first dollar, figure out what everything is going to cost. What the brochure costs, what the printing costs, how much your postage is, what the return reply postage costs, your list costs, and what quantity is involved. Then do another column for all the costs involved in your merchandise, from top to bottom.

As far as pricing goes . . . it has to be competitive. The record business was an existing one and prices were fairly well set in the varied areas. Also, I evaluated what I would be willing to pay for the record my company was putting out. But once you set a price and compare it to all the costs involved, what is your profit margin and where does it fit into anticipated sales?

You may find it's not worth doing a mail-order business. And that's a low blow because you were really anxious to go ahead. However, if it doesn't pay, that's the kind of thing you want to find out before you start, not after you stumble. Then it's too late!

The one real expense is making a classy presentation. You don't have to spend a fortune in terms of a four-color catalogue, but it should be classy. Otherwise, the recipient . . . if you were on the other end, you'd think, what kind of a small outfit is this? What kind of quality do they have?

You've got to spend some money in having the presentation right . . . the photography, the printing . . . it's all a part of selling. Just like the record jacket you see in the store. The customers pick it up to look at because it's a great looking record. Someone is going to pick up your catalogue or brochure to look at the same way. People get so much junk mail that yours has to stand out.

Although all your records are available through mail order and distributors, there's a lot more than the re-issues that you're now involved with. Was that deliberate?

No, not at first. The Comden and Green live recording came about because I was trying to re-issue one of their older recordings. The same thing happened with Liza Minelli and *The Act*. Fred Ebb and John Kander were the show's composers and I had called them in reference to recording some of their songs that had been deleted from old shows. They said "Okay, but how about recording *The Act?*"

For some reason the major companies had neglected the show and both Liza and the composers were anxious to record. So anxious, that some of the normally prohibitive costs to me were worked out in a participation arrangement and we went ahead. It was a fabulous time!

They wanted the record out in three days all across the country, and since my distributors were limited-market suppliers, I licensed it to RCA. So far, it's sold 60,000 copies! In my book, of course, that's a smash.

Not long after . . . so you don't think I'm neglecting my original concept . . . I did an album of Marilyn Monroe, songs that were recorded and never issued on one side, and the soundtrack of *Gentlemen Prefer Blondes* on the other. In one month I sold 8,000 copies! That, to me, was also a smash.

A while back I also produced a cast recording of *Very Good Eddie* at the Goodspeed Opera House and that's been quite successful. I'll be doing an album on Monday with Quentin Crisp and then one with Peggy Lee.

All in all I've done seven albums live and 26 reissues. That makes a total of 33 albums in almost three years.

That's a remarkable accomplishment. At this stage, what percentage of the business is mail order?

About 25 percent. At the same time, that's more profitable, so we're not keeping mail order simply because we started with it. If it didn't pay tomorrow, I'd stop it! Its future is going to be great because I'll have a mail-order business devoted solely to the mail-order customer. Specialized records just for them. They can also take advantage of the commercial releases, but they won't get as great a discount. And I'll keep recording new albums and reissuing the special ones . . . I have enough for another four or five years of reissues.

These records are going to be limited-editions and not available in stores, exclusive to the mail-order customer who is already a part of our philosophy and fully aware of our image in this area. That exclusivity is another incentive for keeping that mail-order customer respectful of what you're doing for him. People write me every day asking if I will be able to get this or that album released. I answer the mail . . . sometimes they give me ideas.

But you will also continue with the recording business . . . like The Act and Peggy Lee?

For sure. But not on a vast scale. I mean it's not as if I want to find a rock group, even though I like rock a lot. Or find a singer. Because that part of the business I don't want . . . the fun is out of it.

How successful has the business been . . . its growth?

It's the past year that has shown the real growth. A year ago it was $65,000 gross. This year, so far, I've grossed $250,000. Since our fiscal year ends in April . . . by that time I might be up to $400,000 because of a couple of deals I made last week.

What about competition in the reissue market . . . your main mail-order thrust?

There has been some. I don't mind competitors. But they have no image and often no concept. They just do a re-release as if that's all there is to it. They pick the wrong ones because they haven't developed their market yet. It's a specialized market . . . not just the record market! They haven't developed the mail-order part of the business. They don't realize that it's built in . . . it's money in your pocket. You're the manufacturer, you're the distributor, you're the seller. It's better than a store. But you have to build an image. You have to answer the mail and service your customers.

We've done a lot of work here. Sometimes it's scary, wondering whether it's going to stop someday. It's not scary to the point of panic or insecurity and it doesn't bother me in the sense of what's going to happen tomorrow if there's no money. That doesn't bother me because I know that every day it's almost like applause from the audience . . . although I never wanted to be an actor . . . when the orders come in or when the re-orders come in, that's it. The re-orders . . . like applause! Then you know that what you've done has been appreciated.

(Hugh Fordin's records are released under the following labels: Out Takes, STET, DRG.)

Success-Steps Analysis

On the surface Hugh Fordin and DRG Records may seem different from the entrepreneurs in the preceding chapters. That's an incorrect assumption, if we think in terms of his small-business profile.

Especially if we remember a few of the small-business prerequisites required by all owner/operators . . . then it's easy to recognize the entrepreneurial similarities they share in common.

- Fordin's personality characteristics reflect the very positive and necessary attributes of drive: motivation and commitment, need and fulfillment, exploration and follow-through.

- There's the essential ingredient of risk and his acceptance of same . . . both in the selection of his products and in the recognition of possible new ways to function or market.

- His ability to rapidly assimilate on-the-job training . . . one of the most valuable methods of acquiring entrepreneurial skills, providing that the "reality experiences" are absorbed with and complemented by additional research.

As we review Fordin's beginner approach to the mail-order aspect of small business, many other commonalities with fellow entrepreneurs are also evident.

Hugh was no exception to a belief held by many advisors and successful owner/managers. Initially, they say, think of getting involved with something you know or like!

Fortunately his great interest in recorded sound and film worked to sharpen his awareness of the potential that might exist in never-published movie outtakes. It served to trigger the thought that there might be other music collectors like himself, who would be interested. Mail order was one of the better ways of locating the actual buyers among them.

Treating it as a sideline venture is an accepted strategy in getting started with mail order . . . an area he knew nothing about! Julian Simon, in his excellent book, *How to Start and Operate a Mail-Order Business,* stresses that it's wise to start part-time. He also notes, "There are no schools in which to learn mail order . . . mostly mail-order people learn by costly experience."

In deciding to go ahead with Out Takes Records, Fordin's moves encompassed many of the established and successful mail-order principles:

- His first product . . . a movie outtake record . . . fit into an existing market of millions of record buyers. Definitely a major market!

- This fact negated the need for him to be a sales pioneer or engage in the heavy marketing research necessary for a completely new product, both of those avenues requiring extensive financial outlays.

- At the same time, his product had an inherent uniqueness and it was not obtainable elsewhere.

- His initial investment and risk factor was modified by only ordering 1,000 records. Along with that, as a sideline venture, there were no meaningful planned expenditures for space, labor, or heavy ads. Dipping the toe in first . . . that's how many mail-order situations start out.

And there are many other well-known trails that were followed by Hugh Fordin, often as a result of common sense rather than structured planning. Rex Reed's column was a smasher and the overwhelming resultant orders a once-in-a-lifetime bonanza! But it proves the small-business maxim of making a strong effort to get free publicity of some kind. A mention, an article, a profile, a review, a sampling, or any combination of same can be extremely effective.

In this case the Reed column's additional bonus was as great as the orders themselves! Because of it, Fordin acquired a large bona fide mailing list of *actual buyers* . . . his own up-to-date list!

An in-house mailing list of buyers is acknowledged by all mail-order pros as better and more profitable than any list you can buy. Hugh Fordin saved years of build-up time, and in combination with his also-fortunate computer arrangement, it set up a strong basis for his future direct-mail offerings.

Another accepted maxim is follow-up . . . capitalize on a successful product by offering something more in the same category or a related one. Volumes 2 and 3 were a continuation and so, in a different sense, were the old album re-issues. The re-issues filled a vacuum and served to actualize the well-known business strategy of . . . "find a need and fill it."

Other recording opportunities were also recognized and then factored into the now-full-time operation, thus starting Hugh's branching out from specialized mail-order to commercial recordings and sales. At the same time everything was put into a well-prepared catalog folio for mail-order merchandising. Within both the commercial and mail-order markets, DRG Records has striven for a specific image and featured a concept that would result in a definitive identity. It also resulted in leadership!

That leadership was achieved from more than just the fact of being first in a specialized field. It began with a unique concept, yes, but it continued with careful, ongoing product selection of re-issues that maintained and furthered a desired image. With that came marketing strategies that embraced a whole series of effective aspects . . . competitive pricing, incentives, fast and responsible UPS deliveries, record review reprints, a well-designed catalog, and finally a soon-to-be exclusive feature of special editions for mail-order buyers only.

A combination of these elements and the established principles mentioned earlier are an important key to Hugh Fordin's present success. They can all be applied, with similar effective results, to any mail-order enterprise . . . especially when product and market are so selectively well-matched.

Mail-Order Overview

Mail order is not for everyone! It is not a simplified, easy way to make a lot of money! For every success, there are hundreds and hundreds of outright failures and many more impatient, flickering fizzles.

There's no question that on the surface it appears to be a very attractive way of starting your own small business. Just look at some of the marvelous pluses:

it can be operated from anywhere
start-up investments can be modest

no age, race, or sex limitations
no face-to-face customer hassles
no need for highly skilled, expensive employees
it can be part-time or full-time
products and markets can be tested without great risk
payments are usually received before shipping

There are other positives. Some use mail order to satisfactorily supplement an existing income. Others start slowly and prepare successfully for a future retirement activity and income. Of paramount importance to many, it can be operated from their own homes, thus saving the expense of separate space, furniture, or a business phone.

Beginners in mail order most often start out on a part-time basis and operate from their homes. Within that framework there is ample opportunity to learn the complex do's and don'ts of this not-so-simple marketing arena. And learn they must! For there are many specialized trade strategies that are unique to this industry.

In addition to becoming familiar with normal and basic business skills, the beginning entrepreneur in mail order has to become aware of the tools, techniques, psychology, and pitfalls that exist. Two highly recommended ways of achieving this awareness are:

- **Study** other mail-order businesses. Read their ads; note the style, layouts, headlines and key appeals. Look through many back issues of specific magazines to see how often the same ads are repeated. Check the mail-order catalogs; get on a list or two and you will be receiving a flock of them. Compare their offerings, prices, and incentives. Talk to other mail-order operators.

- **Read** about mail order. Check books, articles, case histories, or whatever. Check books in the public or educational libraries, bookstores, and associations. With that research you will acquire an awareness and understanding of testing, timing, product acceptability, mailing lists, brokers, ad keys, results-estimating and many, many other industry specifics.

After the initial study and awareness of what mail order might be all about, you have to begin with the actualities.

- Make sure you are a self-starter. Without direct customer interaction, you will have to set the pace. Can you work that way? Are drive and motivation a part of your makeup? Mail-order buildup can be very slow . . . will you stick with it?

- Check the legal requirements. If you use a business name other than your own, check your community's County Clerk office. State and local authorities may require licenses or permits. Zoning regulations may be involved in your residential area. Make sure that your product and your practices are legal and within all government regulations.

- *Capital.* How much to start with? It's true, you can get things moving for a very nominal amount. But small selective magazine ads can be $500 to $800 each and it's rare to be successful with the first one. Direct-mail solicitations, with copy, photos, printing, return order envelopes, list rentals, and postage costs, are even more expensive. Then there are product costs . . . your own or a manufacturer's . . . a minimum order or a drop-ship arrangement. Put them all together; allow for a couple of misses and some costly paid-for experience and the same maxim for all business holds true—don't under-capitalize! You may need 10 or $15,000 for that initial healthy start, depending upon product selection and marketing avenues. Much cheaper than opening a store, but it still means you should know as much as possible about your operation *before* you start. By choosing classifieds and/or the non-top rated (but highly effective) magazines, you may minimize your initial investment and marketing tests . . . also, the cost of your first learning experiences.

- Product selection is often the biggest stumbling block in setting up a mail-order operation. In many cases it's still difficult for an existing one. It is, however, the key to the business . . . it sets up the how, where, and why of all your marketing strategies. And it has to fit into a lot of evaluative criteria, especially in a first-time start-out.

Don't pick a product that is readily available in stores, or one that is already featured in a number of mail-order catalogs.

Make sure your product is targeted toward a major market or large segment of the population (for example, fishermen, drivers, homemakers, executives).

Is it trouble-free? If it can easily fail or be subject to servicing and replacement, the returns, requests for refunds, and customer complaints can wipe you out. Present sales and possible future sales to the same customer are both lost.

Is it easily mailable? Check-points here are perishability, fragility, size, and weight. Excesses in any of these areas can increase forwarding and packaging costs . . . sometimes to the point of negating the item's profitability.

Can it be a profitable item? The quoted price must seem reasonable for the product. Unlike retail stores, mail order often requires a price factor of three to four times the total product cost to you. This is needed to cover product and delivery charges from your supplier; packaging; shipping; selling costs (advertising, mail, et cetera); and overhead. A lesser markup can be applied if the product is one of many in a catalog or in a multi-item circular mailing.

Is it a one-shot item or does it have repeat sales potential? Repeat sale items . . . products that are consumed or used up . . . can create a steady demand, thus lowering the need for the higher markup. Reorders don't require any new sales effort and profits are greater, therefore that type of product is most desirable. Admittedly, it may take time to develop and build this type of operation.

One-shot items are what most people envision in mail order. It succeeds or fails quickly. At the same time there's big money if it goes over and not too big a loss if it fails. Problems? Of course. Success will immediately breed competitors who will help skim the top cream off, so you have to keep coming up with new ideas or fads to keep going.

Is your product easily advertised? Simply stated, products that are easy to illustrate with pictures or sketches and/or easy to describe with copy, are the best for marketing purposes. Too much copy, complex explanations, or needed demonstration can make ad costs too expensive.

Don't start with a completely new product . . . follow other products that have proven successful. They have already proved that a market exists, that the product is an accepted one, and the specific media employed was effective. This belief is shared by many proponents of mail order, as well as by existing operators. It doesn't mean that you cannot be successful with a new and unique item . . . but the record shows that winners are few.

For a newcomer to the field, an initial "copy cat" theme is best. It can save the heavy expense of trial and error, the often-elusive search for a satisfactory market, and the sometimes overwhelming rigors of being first.

- Finally, get started. That means another batch of decisions have to be made. Do you solicit by mail or use advertisements? If ads are the answer, what media do you select? What about testing before you go all-out, testing price, ads, copy, media, and the product itself?

Remember, no one said it was easy. It's just that everyone thinks it is! What's above is just the bare beginning. Good luck.

9 Why Not Franchising?

The last time William Shapiro had anything to do with a small business was in a partnership, way back in 1951.

After that there were a number of years as a cabbie in New York City and finally the westward trek to Phoenix, Arizona.

Although successful in his last job, William sensed that something was missing and at 56 he made a major move.

From that point on, he went back full circle into a small business of his own . . . this time with his wife, Mollie Shapiro, as a partner.

BASKIN-ROBBINS ICE CREAM STORE * PHOENIX, ARIZONA

William and Mollie Shapiro's franchised store is located on North Central Avenue and Camelback Road. It is a historical unit among the many around the nation.

Built in 1959, it was the first Baskin-Robbins store ever franchised out of the state of California. It's been refurbished and up-dated a number of times since, although the parking area for it and the other stores connected alongside is quite meager.

Bill, you've been in Phoenix over 25 years. Why didn't you go into business when you first arrived?

When I came here in 1962, things were very quiet. They were so quiet, I used to call it a depressed area. Everything was overbuilt. Gas stations, homes, supermarkets; everybody was anticipating the big growth here, but it hadn't happened yet. And wages were low.

I just felt I didn't want to go into anything at that time because it seemed depressed. So I figured I'd work a while and I did. After New York it took me a long time to get used to Phoenix.

In the past eight or ten years, of course, Arizona and the Southwest have been booming. Did that make the difference?

Well, partly. I was working at J.C. Penney for eight years before I went into business. I was quite happy there and did pretty well. Then I started to feel like I was missing something. I guess I just got a little bored with the job.

Seeing the growth in Phoenix, it seemed I could use my talents in my own business. My position in Penney's was selling major appliances, and I was pretty successful in doing that. One day I just happened to mention to one of my sons that I was interested in going into business. He suggested a Baskin-Robbins franchise because he knew someone who had one.

What were the other reasons that influenced you? Any bad vibes on the job?

Oh, no, nothing like that. You see, we have four children, three boys and a girl, and they were all gone from the house. Going away to college, getting married, and so on. We were all alone. Well, I just felt that I didn't want to sit home every night watching television with my wife on the couch.

When I approached Mollie with the idea, she was lukewarm. But Joel, my oldest son, looked into the franchise idea a bit and he thought it was very good. My wife had never worked before and I told her it was *not* my intention to start a mom and pop business. Anyway, I sent an application into Baskin-Robbins. We waited about a year before I could buy this store.

Why did it take so long?

It took a year until a store came up that was suitable for me. Sometimes you can put in an application and there are stores already available for sale. At the time I applied, nothing was for sale and we just had to wait it out.

We kept in touch with Baskin-Robbins all that time, and one day they said they expected three stores to be available. This was one of them.

Before we go ahead with that, can you tell me why you picked the franchise idea? Why Baskin-Robbins?

I did have some business background from many years ago. I was a fur manufacturer in New York and my partner decided to leave after being together for six years. Since the business was speculative, I went out of it the same time he did. Then, later, I purchased a taxi medallion and I was still my own boss, so to speak.

But those experiences were completely different from what I might get into in Phoenix, and they were a long time ago, too. A franchise seemed a good idea because it can give a lot of backup in areas I didn't know enough about.

Baskin-Robbins made a lot of sense. They had an excellent, well-known product. They had a success story . . . in business for something like 34 years. I figured they didn't get there just because of their name. They did something! Maybe it was know-how . . . or a good marketing program . . . or whatever.

Mollie, how did you really feel about all this . . . three years ago?

I guess I *was* skeptical. Bill had never been in a retail business before and I was concerned that there would be long hours involved, not much chance for us to spend time together.

I wasn't worried about the financial end because I knew that Bill could do a good job in whatever he set out to do. At the same time, if the decision was to be a franchise business, Baskin-Robbins was okay with me. It was acceptable because it had a very good name, a quality product, and it was known everywhere.

Even though I wasn't sure at the time, it seemed like a good possibility.

Getting back to the beginning, Bill. After the application for the franchise, what was the next step?

They interviewed me . . . and Mollie was a part of it also. I filled out a financial statement at first. Then there was a questionnaire about why I wanted to get into the business, why I *felt* I wanted to get into it. How I thought I could get along with youngsters and the younger generation.

They covered a lot of other areas, too. They usually recommend a family-run operation. Anyway, they felt I was qualified.

What about training? Was that just before you took over the store?

Right. After the purchase, there was a three-week training period at their school in Burbank, California. The travel, hotel, and food costs were at my expense but not the school. That's how Mollie got involved.

I asked her to go to school with me, to keep me company for the three weeks. We could drive there together and it would be an enjoyable trip. She agreed. But I still have to say that neither of us, at the time, were thinking about her working in the store.

How did it go? What did the training consist of?

First we had classroom study about the business end of it. Naturally, the bookkeeping, suggestions for ways of doing and understanding the bookkeeping systems. The buying of supplies and the purchasing of the product. Marketing programs.

Afterwards we had field study . . . going to their own stores. They assigned us stores in the evening and we had to go there and work behind the counter. Previous to that, however, we had morning sessions . . . before the stores were open. There were two hours in the morning where they taught us how to make sundaes, decorate a cake, and so on.

We went through the whole routine of how to work the equipment, how to maintain it, how to clean it, what to expect. We were assigned to various jobs throughout the store. It was excellent.

And, I've got to admit, it paid off. When I stepped into my own store that first morning, I was able to come in and just do everything.

Mollie, what about your training? How did it go with you?

The first week was so-so. Bookkeeping and that sort of thing, it's not my bag. But the second week, when we started to work in the Baskin-Robbins stores, that was really enjoyable.

I found it to be fun and I loved relating to people. That's when I decided, then and there, to work with my husband. I had never worked outside my home before . . . I was always too busy taking care of Bill, my family, and my home.

It's been almost three years now and I've never regretted that decision. I still enjoy every minute of it.

> **Bill, you closed the deal for the store before you took the training course. Can you give me the details, the price, the actual steps involved?**

The franchisor in the Phoenix area for Baskin-Robbins gave me the figures for this particular unit. The price for the store was $63,000 plus approximately $4,000 in inventory. There was something like 29 percent down and notes for five years for the remainder. The down payment, by the way, was not borrowed money.

The inventory is important because when we take over, business continues right on the *next day.* The night before we took over, at closing time, Baskin-Robbins representatives came in and took a total inventory for the former owner. It took about a month to figure out what I owed the previous owner and then it was paid out to him a month or two later.

There were closing charges, too, a transfer fee of $1,700 and the security for the first and last months' rent. And there's a lot of paper work involved.

> **Did you have a lawyer for that? And an accountant to check the books?**

No, I didn't have a lawyer. Everything takes place at the Baskin-Robbins headquarters in Phoenix . . . all the signing, inventory reports, and gross business. In fact, another owner, who had a lawyer, said he didn't feel he even needed one. He said it was a waste of money.

I knew what the bottom line in the books said, because Baskin-Robbins had the records of all the ice-cream purchases made by the former owner. Also his sales were reported every month. They can estimate exactly what your returns should be and how well you're dishing out the product.

That may work out if it's a reputable franchisor. But all franchise situations should be checked carefully. You said earlier that you started operating the next day . . . what about experienced help, working capital, supplies, et cetera?

You do start with the existing employees, supervise them for a while, and then you keep whom you want. Later you hire others and train them. When I went to their school, we picked up suggestions on how to train and that's something I take care of now.

As far as cash flow goes . . . it starts to come in as soon as you open the door! We knew how much volume we were going to be doing, so it's an immediate thing. Although you don't need a big start-up fund, there should always be a little extra money for the larger bills that come up.

Your insurance, for example, may average out to $100 a month, but you may get a bill for a semi-annual premium right away. So you should have some operational capital available.

What about supplies? Do you have to buy everything from the franchiser?

The ice-cream products—yes! I wouldn't have it any other way, because of their 100 percent quality. That's why I chose Baskin-Robbins in the first place.

For paper goods, syrups, and various other needs, we have suppliers. They cater to the Baskin-Robbins people and keep up with the required specifications and expected quality.

My rent, by the way, goes to Baskin-Robbins. They have a separate company that has all the leases to all the stores. We sub-lease from them.

This type of operation requires plenty of hours. Is there a mandated time schedule? And how do you handle the whole setup?

Yes, there are mandated hours and it's a seven-day operation. The only day they really allow you to close is Christmas. But they don't enforce it too heavily. On Thanksgiving, half a day is enough.

Our hours in the summer are from 10:00 AM to 10:30 or 11:00 PM. In the winter usually from 11:00 AM. It's a lot of hours and we keep about five or six in help to manage the time.

Usually one of us is here with the employees . . . my wife in the evenings. I'm on the day shift. Mollie works five nights a week and we have somebody who's reliable to take up the slack.

Does Mollie help with the books, the details?

No, that's not her thing. She loves to stay out there with the people. And she has a reputation. A lot of people just come in to talk with her. They pass up other places just to come here.

The reporter from our local paper said it best. Here, take a look at this article: "Mollie, who 'treats people the way I want to be treated,' has a following who bring her gifts and happily forfeit their place in line, 'so Mollie can wait on me.' "

That's the great way it is with Mollie. I do the bookkeeping. I make my own payroll and pay the bills. We have a bookkeeper who comes in and gives me a monthly profit-and-loss statement. He combines my whole month's business into a booklet. And each month it comes back to me with a total picture of the previous month's business.

Franchises are usually quite structured and, in a sense, that means you're not alone. Have you found this to be true?

Oh, yes. We have district representatives who come around occasionally. If you need anything, or have a problem, all you do is call them and they come over to help you out.

The company also has quarterly meetings. We owners get together and go over the program for the next three months and see all the new marketing ideas. The marketing area program tells us everything to expect in the way of new flavors for the next quarter, specials, et cetera. And we receive a booklet that covers it all.

We also get a report every month of how we are standing among the other stores. It tells us what the average increase or decrease has been for the month for the whole state of Arizona. This gives you an idea of how you are doing.

What about advertising? Do they take care of it all or do you handle the local type?

We can. We have certain layouts available, which we can use individually in the local papers and penny savers. But most of it is done through our getting together and putting the program of advertising in ourselves.

Of course, there's national advertising. That has nothing to do with this store . . . we don't pay for national.

That's right. I think Baskin-Robbins is one of the few franchisors that doesn't impose a franchise fee, a royalty percentage, or a national advertising charge.

Yes, I think so. Someone did say the franchise fee, or something like it, is built into the costs for the initial equipment and layout, et cetera. And I guess a royalty is not needed when the whole idea is to buy all the product from them. All that's been okay with me.

You mentioned that your gross sales for the first year was up to par . . . in the area of $117,000. Did that work out okay? How did the business do after that?

The first year did live up to our expectations . . . somewhere in that area of gross sales. We certainly are passing that in the second year. We've had a price increase of 10 percent recently and that will be reflected in sales.

But that's not the only reason for our growth. Previously, the store was under absentee ownership, because the owner had three stores. There's no question that if it's run by the owners themselves, as we are doing, business will increase a great deal.

That newspaper article that mentioned Mollie also indicated that you had gross sales of near $140,000. Is that where it's going? What about profits?

Yes. I guess it could go that and above. As far as net profit goes, Baskin-Robbins recommends that it should run about 20 percent. Your gross profit, after the cost of ice cream, should be in the neighborhood of 60 percent. After that, all your expenses come off . . . salaries, paper goods, insurance, rent, and utilities.

Do you and Mollie take salaries? Or do you take a draw and then bonuses, as available?

We take a draw. Enough to live comfortably and pay expenses. No bonuses, really. I'd rather leave it in to pay the taxes and everything. Don't forget, I'm still paying off notes every month, for five years.

Do you think a franchise is too cut and dried, too structured . . . no room for independent thinking? That's what bothers some people.

It depends on a lot of things. If you haven't been in business before, it's a very good way to go. You have all that structure and experience to back you up, to help you out in the areas you don't know. That strict routine is what a franchise is all about . . . you should know that and accept it, going in, and you won't be frustrated. There isn't much room for striking out on your own. If that's what you want, forget a franchise.

They've made all the mistakes and done all the research and the experimenting. When you start a small business from scratch, it takes a few years to get going, just to know if you are going to succeed or fail. And most of them fail! Also . . . you have to live for those few years, and that can be tough when you're building up from the bottom.

Naturally, the franchise has to be a reputable one . . . you have to really check it out. There are plenty with problems, on *both* sides.

In a sense, it's a more controlled operation and therefore easier to identify the trouble areas.

True. Let's take a simple thing like how you pack ice cream. We usually have a 2½-ounce scoop to make a profit. If you're going to give too much ice cream on a cone, naturally you're going to decrease your profits. So a *healthy* 2½-ounce scoop is what we're looking for most of the time.

Some do it properly; some overscoop. You've just got to keep training them, make them scoop every day to practice more and more. It's a knack.

Every Monday morning we also take what we call a "flash gross profit figure inventory." From that inventory, we have a way of figuring by ratio whether the ice cream is being handled properly, whether we're overscooping or not. It *is* more systematized, but, as you said, it's also a big help in spotting problems.

To get back to the human side of things, how do you and Mollie get along? Not seeing much of each other?

First of all Mollie usually works five nights a week and I'm still up when she gets home. I usually take a day off anyway. And we're also home a couple of evenings a week together. We haven't found it to be a problem. Besides which, we're talking to each other all day on the phone.

Mollie, why did you take the night shift rather than daytime hours?

Basically, I'm a night person. It's also a question of how I like to do things. It's important to me to have my home cleaned and ship-shape before I get started on other projects. The combination of having everything done at home and leaving a prepared dinner for Bill worked out best for the night shift. The hours I put in are also shorter than the day shift.

And don't forget my regulars. We enjoy a good visit together in the evenings . . . there's a lot of activity then and I really like meeting people. As Bill says, "This is a happy business."

There's another benefit, too. A lot of the paperwork can be done in the day hours, and Bill can interview and train new personnel during that time. In the afternoon the store isn't as busy as it is at other times and that's when all the training should take place.

Mollie, what about your sons? I heard earlier that they were interested in a Baskin-Robbins unit for themselves.

That's true. Both Robert and Edward are college graduates in the liberal arts and there isn't too much you can do in business with that kind of background. If they really want to start a business, the franchise idea would make a lot of sense. This one is a clean kind of situation with a quality product and, as an added bonus, they do have some experience in it.

Bill: Yes, Robert's presently finishing his thesis for his Master's. In the meantime he's been working for Bullock's department store in Tempe. He lives there and has come over to help me out occasionally. Edward lives in Tucson.

They're thinking of buying an existing store in Tucson together. I don't think I would advise them to buy one individually, because it's very difficult to get reliable people to take over when you're not there. I don't care to operate that way, although many other owners do.

You both seem pleased with what you're doing and what you've accomplished. Has everything worked out the way you expected?

Mollie and I are very happy with the Baskin-Robbins operation. They were honest and very fair with me. They tried to help me in every way. And they're not trying to take every nickel that you have. Everything they promised to do, was done.

They allow you to make your profit, although this isn't any easy road to becoming wealthy. It's no way to make a great deal of money. Maybe some people are looking for higher profits. If they are, then this is not the business for them.

But we're happy with it. And don't kid yourself . . . if you want to make anything out of a business, you have to work hard. If you try to take advantage of the public by making your percentage of return too high, you're not going to make it. So the way they taught us and the way we operate, it came out very nice and we're very happy with it. If this wasn't a product that we liked, my wife and I could never sell it . . . not with any sincerity or enthusiasm.

Success-Steps Analysis

Because he traveled a different route into entrepreneurship, you might think that our lessons from William Shapiro's moves would be different. This is not true. We can still review the positive moves he made in becoming an entrepreneur.

In noting the similarities that exist among some of the other interviewed small-business owners, there are a number of factors that coincide with Bill Shapiro's own outlook:

- Once he decided to enter the arena of owning a small business, his commitment was firm.

- The thought of hard work and a seven-day week did not dissuade him.

- His willingness to enter an ownership area completely dissimilar from his other experiences confirmed the risk factor that is so mandatory.

- The use of his own capital for the 29 percent down payment also reflected the risk aspect.

- The reasoning that made him choose a franchise indicated the kind of perception required for a good "business sense."

- By entering that new field, he acknowledged and accepted the need for a learning experience, through structured training.

And there are other facets that come into positive play in relation to Bill's ownership venture. A franchise involving so many mandated hours obviously required employees . . . not somewhere in the future, but the very day he opened for customer service. His personality, therefore, must be suitable to handle that relationship aspect, and employee training as well.

A pleasant personality and a great deal of patience were also prime requisites . . . both from a pure retail viewpoint and also because of the youngsters that were a big part of his buying public. William Shapiro, in making his decision for a Baskin-Robbins ice-cream store, must have evaluated his own character for coping in that environment. Apparently it wasn't found to be lacking, measured by the past three years of successful operation.

Although his selection of a Baskin-Robbins franchise seemed quite casual and without intensive research, it wasn't quite that easy-going. His common-sense reasoning directed him toward some logical conclusions:

- There was *some* business background in his past, but it was over a quarter of a century ago.

- His recent retail sales experience in major appliances confirmed his ability to get along with the buying public even though he had *no* knowledge of handling, buying, pricing, advertising, and other varied management practices.

- At his age he didn't want to struggle for years to build up a business from scratch . . . his real purpose was to simply become more involved.

- New businesses were a tremendous risk; he had been warned that the great majority fail within the first two years.

- An existing business would make sense, but it still meant acquiring all the necessary business and management skills . . . alone.

- A franchise operation would make more sense because it would back him up in all the management areas that he was not sufficiently exposed to in his sales job.

Of course, it didn't end there. Which franchise to select can involve a great amount of study and research. Maybe Bill Shapiro didn't do enough of that . . . but his initial criteria were certainly impressive. Baskin-Robbins fit the bill in many areas that would concern him. Their assets were numerous:

> nationally known
> nationally advertised
> established over 30 years
> one of the largest in its field
> over 1700 stores
> a quality product
> a "clean" situation
> a still-growing consumer acceptance
> a good marketing program

In addition, both Bill and Mollie honestly liked the taste and quality of the ice-cream products. They also were favorably impressed by the reputation of the company. All in all, it was a good start in his attempt to finalize a business selection. A glaring omission, it should be noted, was his not using an independent attorney to check the contract and attend the signing.

Later, however, when he could evaluate everything by actualities rather than suppositions, his conclusions were positive ones. The three-week training enabled him to walk right into his own business and start operating. The buying, pricing, advertising, and inventory control skills that he learned were just the kind of backup that he needed. It enabled him to quickly study a new field and be able to handle it confidently, while getting more on-the-job training and experience.

Fortunately Mollie Shapiro, who had never worked before, was immediately attracted to the situation and proved to be one of Bill's greatest assets. One of his other assets has to do with his understanding and acceptance of what a franchise is all about. Why it must have rules of operation and *structured* procedures that must be adhered to . . . he made that a positive factor in his operation, not a negative. To many others, it may prove to be too restrictive.

He also warned that if you go the franchise route, it must be the right franchise . . . well-checked, with a good reputation. Baskin-Robbins was right for him. It may not be for everybody!

Franchise Facts

Franchises today are an important segment of our small-business ownership. Of the more than 500,000 outlets that exist, the very great majority are independently operated by franchisees.

Over the years there have been plenty of problems and fraudulent practices in this still-growing field. Promises of quick and ready profits, easy hours, instant entrepreneurship, and low beginner capital, were the lures to many a rip-off. All too often the inference was that "anyone can be a success" and, as a result, those totally unqualified to cope with a business entered the failure arena.

Is the situation better now? Definitely so, but the old cautions still apply. Anyone contemplating a franchise must thoroughly *check it out,* investigate and research the franchisor and its record. This means the franchisor's reputation, capabilities, agreements, the territories, existing units, restriction . . . *everything* about it!

The very fact that many state and federal agencies have in the last few years passed a number of laws relating to the governing of franchises, is indicative of the need to approach these operations carefully.

The Federal Trade Commission (FTC) notes that they get thousands of letters every year from people who complain that they have been victimized by franchise operators. Although they usually involve small franchisors, the complaints relate to areas that should be scrutinized in any franchise operation:

> the profit potential was exaggerated
> the supplies were overpriced
> the training was insufficient
> too little technical assistance was offered
> their territory was not protected

Promises for all these aspects were made, but not carried through or, in some cases, were completely falsified.

The FTC, as a result of many abuses, formulated rules that became effective July 21, 1979. Franchise operators will be required to give the following information to potential investors:

(1) A list of all key executives in the franchise operation and their employment background.

(2) Disclosure of all lawsuits and bankruptcies in which the company has been involved.

(3) Disclosure of all suppliers that the franchisee has to do business with, and the amounts of money these suppliers pay to the franchise operator.

(4) A full description of any financial assistance given by the franchisor to the franchisee.

(5) Disclosure of all the money a franchisee has to pay—both at the start and during the life of the business.

(6) A clear explanation of the terms under which the franchise may be revoked.

Many states have franchise-disclosure laws that relate to similar areas of the FTC regulations. Take another look at those rules and read them carefully. They give you a real overview of exactly where some of those questionable franchisors tried to hold back vital information. The kind of information that could spell the difference between running a successful business or being caught in an ever-struggling, never-quite-making-it faulty operation. And some of those same information areas were glossed over by the larger franchisors. It pays to be aware of the problem spots that may crop up.

During the past decade the squeeze has been put on many of the questionable and incapable franchisors . . . and they've been dropping out of the industry. Hopefully, this trend will continue until the remaining well-financed, capably-run franchisors are in the great majority. Since this field is still growing, however, and since almost anything in services, products, or distribution can be put into the franchise mold, the watchwords will be the same. Investigate and check it out before you commit yourself.

There are a few other areas often overlooked by those who try to investigate a franchise opportunity. One is not spending time with those who already operate a unit in the franchise being considered. That's where you can discover where the problems lie and where the real potentials exist. This should be done with people you select at random, and not with those who are set up for interviews by the franchisor.

Secondly, check yourself out! Is scooping ice cream seven days a week something you can see yourself doing? Is a retail operation . . . dealing with the public all day . . . an experience you can handle? Will you want to work that franchise for ten or fifteen years—if that's what the contract calls for? Of course, not all questions can be easily answered. That's why it's also advisable to spend some time with those people already in the business of your choice. You may be able to find out what it's really like.

There's plenty of information about the franchise field available . . . in libraries, government agencies, books, and through the franchise associations. It's well worth studying some of this material, specifically with the purpose of increasing your awareness of the complexities that exist in this field.

The Department of Commerce publishes a frequently updated reference book, *Franchise Opportunities Handbook,* which includes a listing and brief summary of over 900 franchisors. It can be purchased from the Superintendent of Documents, U.S. Government Printing Office, Washington, DC, 20402, or at any Government Bookstore.

Within that book is an excellent checklist of 25 questions relating to the evaluation of a franchise opportunity. It was prepared by Dr. Wilford L. White, and is reprinted here.

Checklist for Evaluating a Franchise

The Franchise

1. Did your lawyer approve the franchise contract you are considering after he studied it paragraph by paragraph?
2. Does the franchise call upon you to take any steps which are, according to your lawyer, unwise or illegal in your state, county or city?
3. Does the franchise give you an exclusive territory for the length of the franchise or can the franchisor sell a second or third franchise in your territory?
4. Is the franchisor connected in any way with any other franchise company handling similar merchandise or services?
5. If the answer to the last question is "yes" what is your protection against this second franchisor organization?
6. Under what circumstances can you terminate the franchise contract and at what cost to you, if you decide for any reason at all that you wish to cancel it?
7. If you sell your franchise, will you be compensated for your good will or will the good will you have built into the business be lost by you?

The Franchisor

8. For how many years has the firm offering you a franchise been in operation?
9. Has it a reputation for honesty and fair dealing among the local firms holding its franchise?
10. Has the franchisor shown you any certified figures indicating exact net profits of one or more going firms which you personally checked yourself with the franchisee?
11. Will the firm assist you with:
    (a) A management training program?
    (b) An employee training program?
    (c) A public relations program?
    (d) Capital?
    (e) Credit?
    (f) Merchandising ideas?
12. Will the firm assist you in finding a good location for your new business?
13. Is the franchising firm adequately financed so that it can carry out its stated plan of financial assistance and expansion?

14. Is the franchisor a one man company or a corporation with an experienced management trained in depth (so that there would always be an experienced man at its head)?
15. Exactly what can the franchisor do for you which you cannot do for yourself?
16. Has the franchisor investigated you carefully enough to assure itself that you can successfully operate one of their franchises at a profit both to them and to you?
17. Does your state have a law regulating the sale of franchises and has the franchisor complied with that law?

You—The Franchisee

18. How much equity capital will you have to have to purchase the franchise and operate it until your income equals your expenses? Where are you going to get it?
19. Are you prepared to give up some independence of action to secure the advantages offered by the franchise?
20. Do YOU really believe you have the innate ability, training, and experience to work smoothly and profitably with the franchisor, your employees, and your customers?
21. Are you ready to spend much or all of the remainder of your business life with this franchisor, offering his product or service to your public?

Your Market

22. Have you made any study to determine whether the product or service which you propose to sell under franchise has a market in your territory at the prices you will have to charge?
23. Will the population in the territory given you increase, remain static, or decrease over the next 5 years?
24. Will the product or service you are considering be in greater demand, about the same, or less demand 5 years from now than today?
25. What competition exists in your territory already for the product or service you contemplate selling?
    (a) Nonfranchise firms?
    (b) Franchise firms?

10 The "Professionals"

When the soon-to-be-an-entrepreneur begins to fill in the boxes that represent starting costs, he or she usually hesitates to fill in the ones relating to professional fees.

"Can I get along without them . . . at the start, anyway?"

That kind of thinking is absolutely normal at this stage, for the beginner has had no previous experience with which to evaluate this need. At the same time, this lack of practical knowledge often results in a lack of confidence in the advice that is forthcoming from these kinds of consultations.

Then add to that an unfamiliarity with what each of the professional's advice actually means in concrete help for the beginner . . . and you start to get questions. Perhaps the professionals should answer themselves.

PEOPLE TO CONSULT

Planning to start a small business often involves many areas that the beginner has *no* experience with or knowledge about. These can include the complexities of pricing, inventory, marketing, buying, advertising, and a dozen other areas.

And then there are the additional brain twisters: "Shall I incorporate? Is this lease okay? *What* am I supposed to file and with whom? If I get a partner, how do I protect myself?"

While you're wrestling with the needs of furniture and fixtures, inventory, et cetera, there are more problems in the question-and-answer realm. "Records? Taxes? Wait a minute, I haven't even started. Why do I need liability insurance? Do I have to use all my own money . . . can't I get a loan?"

Let's hope that you've been doing your research prior to starting out. Reading non-stop, perhaps, wherever those business mysteries and brain-twisters exist. Probing trade association materials, attending seminars, and maybe talking with others in the same industry. There's no end to the sources that can help to illuminate . . . at least partly.

All is not lost, however—if you use "the professionals." Consult and/or hire the lawyer, accountant, banker, insurance broker, wherever it's necessary . . . especially at the inception. Some entrepreneurs who have been over this route and are now established agree wholeheartedly. Others indicate that they certainly are helpful but, at the same time, don't treat them as the final word . . . it's your own decision-making that counts.

If you have taken the time to read and research . . . if you've acquired *some* understanding of these previously unknown areas . . . then you will be able to follow and evaluate the professional's advice. Factor that advice into your own thinking and beliefs, then go ahead and make the decision.

With that viewpoint in mind, it seemed logical to mini-interview the professionals. Listen to the ideas they think would be relevant to a beginning venture and, at the same time, let them indicate where and how they can help the small business start-up.

Bank Executive: First National Bank—Tucson, Arizona

What do you look for in the person who requests a loan to start a small business?

First of all, we want to know something about the person, their background and abilities. Second of all, what the business is and how they intend to capitalize it . . . what type of entity it's going to be and why it's going to be that particular type of organizational structure. We want as much information as possible, so that we can understand the business.

Should they have a formal business plan or merely the answers to the questions you just asked?

One of the most important considerations in a new enterprise is the quality of management. We don't have any specific requirements for the submission of a detailed plan for the business. But when they do submit one, it's indicative of their ability. If a fully-prepared plan is submitted, it's a lot more impressive than if we have to hold their hand and carry them through the entire project.

Start-up loans are difficult to obtain from a bank unless there is both ample capital investment and experience in the proposed project. Any comment that would help clarify this?

Start-up loans are probably the highest-risk loans to make. Our business, in all fairness to our depositors, does not involve high-risk situations. At the same time, we are not investors . . . we are creditors, and there's a big distinction between the two. Many customers do have a hard time understanding that difference. We are not in for the risk-return, we are in for getting our money repaid at a reasonable rate of interest-return. With those factors in consideration, it isn't difficult to understand why new business start-up loans are almost impossible to grant.

Bank Officer/SBA Loans: First National Bank—Tucson, Arizona

Many new entrepreneurs think that the SBA bank participation loans are the easy answer to their financial start-up requirements. Is that fantasy thinking?

There are quite a few who come in with that idea in mind. They feel that with an SBA loan guarantee, the money is 90 percent guaranteed to the bank, so why should the bank care . . . what's a small 10 percent of risk? So in their opinion it's relatively no risk. Therefore they expect the bank to be as enthusiastic and optimistic about their loan request as they are.

It's really a shock for them to find out that we actually treat their SBA guaranteed loan request just like any other regular loan request. The only difference is that if we see a lot of potential in their venture, but it's still not strong enough for the bank's direct loan, then we will ask the SBA to look over the package. If they agree with us, and they more than likely will, then they do guarantee 90 percent of that loan request.

You mentioned a "lot of potential." What does that mean from the bank's viewpoint?

Since we're not in the business of high risk, it means making sure that the type of venture has a probability of acceptance and success. That there does exist both managerial and operational capabilities on the part of the would-be entrepreneur. And that there is the proper capital to get into it.

As you pointed out, all those factors may still not be strong enough for a direct, bank loan . . . Does the SBA program require that same kind of in-depth potential?

Oh, yes. In effect their 90 percent guarantee loan grant requires the exact same information that ours does. I've also seen the SBA turn down loan requests because they felt the applicants had not utilized all of their own assets, to the extent that the SBA loan was not required. In other cases of secondary collateral, they may not ask you to refinance your house, but they will put a second deed against it. Then if the new business does go under, they will work something out with you at that time to repay the loan . . . refinance the mortgage, sell the house, et cetera.

Do many people who come in for an SBA guaranteed loan qualify?

It varies, but most are turned down. Some of them are very, very far-fetched. Others we tell to go back and do their homework . . . get some proforma balance sheets, see if they really want to get involved in their own small business. If so, they can come back for us to take another look.

There will be a few who have gone to an organization that puts together an SBA loan package. Here's one of those, for a restaurant—a large $200,000 loan. It's very well put together, with complete data, backgrounds, proformas, projections, and so on. Over 250 pages. Many of these pages are not relevant, but they felt the SBA might require them.

That's okay for that kind of operation. But most potential entrepreneurs of small businesses can't project accurately, make pro-forma's, P and L's, et cetera, even with an accountant.

That information is a must for the banks and the SBA in order to analyze the success potential of the loan. Of equal importance, it's vital for the applicant . . . for he has to know where he's going, what's going to happen in the future. When everything is figured out, the costs may exceed the revenues and the net result is that it should not have been started in the first place.

The key thing we should all be looking at is the reality of the figures—how were the projected sales based, where did the figures come from, have they been taken from the industry itself, the local area itself?

Anyone can go to their bank and ask what are the various average ratios for that specific type of industry. They usually have RMA annual statement studies that show the key ratios of a financial statement . . . both the balance sheet and the income statement . . . for many industries. That's why we can readily judge a loan request for an existing business; comparing their previous history of sales, expenses, net income, cash flow, et cetera, with typical ratios in each category. This determines the ability to repay the loan.

When you're looking at a start-up loan request, however, you have nothing to go on. To a bank, that's high-risk. We don't normally make that type of loan. But if we do review that type of loan, we have to feel certain that the pro-forma figures for a two-year period are realistic. The true values are important. That's where the homework comes in.

Costs, expenses, sales . . . were they pulled out of a hat? Were the actual range of salaries, utilities, and expenses of that local area checked out? Were *industry* sales researched? Were businesses of the size proposed investigated, talked to, analyzed? If these types of figures were gathered, then a realistic pro-forma could be structured by the applicant with the help of an accountant. In any event, this should be a requirement for the bank and the SBA, as well as for the future owner/manager of the small business.

Bank Officer: Manufacturers Hanover Trust—New York, N.Y.

Even though a start-up loan may not be possible, is it still advisable for the person planning a small business to discuss financing and "things business" with a banker?

Definitely yes. In practice, of course, there may be a problem in the amount of time the banker can spare. This is especially true when the potential beginner hasn't done his homework and is simply looking for *free advice*. An accountant or a lawyer would charge a fee.

The banker does not charge because we are devoting that time to build up a relationship. It works best, of course, when the future entrepreneur has already done some research, some planning, and is somewhat knowledgeable about the specific questions that need clarification. Then, even if time is short, a number of the financing mysteries can be answered and an accountant or some other business person can be recommended by the banker for additional assistance. In the New York City area, for example, we might suggest taking advantage of the free counseling services offered by the volunteer retired executives organization.

You mentioned "financing mysteries." What does this mean in relation to the start-up situation?

Our past experience has shown that many who wish to start a business are somewhat weak in the areas of finance. We'll have someone who has a great idea, a lot of enthusiasm, a clientele that seems to be just waiting for this product . . . now the question of production comes up. Well, he does have someone who will give him terms on the supplies that are necessary and someone else who will produce a small amount to get him started.

That's great, but realistic production is another matter! He's talking about something that's going to require hundreds of customers to be successful and all he's providing for, at this moment, are two or three clients. This is when a number of questions start coming up. How do you provide production for the hundreds of customers that will be needed? How do you give terms to the two or three clients—and they will want terms—who are starting you off? How do you get the capital for these very normal situations? This is when the discussion must turn to financing, to adequate capitalization, to cash flow.

In another instance, a terrific salesman or great designer for a large corporation decides to go into their own business. Usually they are thoroughly familiar with only *one aspect* of that business. The former customers are willing to stick with the new outfit and send their orders in. You can't beat that for a start.

But if problems develop, it's no longer a big corporation's responsibility . . . it's the new entrepreneur's tough luck. In production . . . the supplies may be late; the mold may be sticking; the material has developed flaws; or the original material was not available and a substitute had to be used. Perhaps, additionally, favorable credit terms are non-existent.

Late deliveries can result in cancellations and, in some cases, there may be returns for any number of reasons. All of these factors are possible and any one or two of them can create a crisis of finance for a new start-up situation. Most beginners have no financial reserve and they often start out under-capitalized. It's not a "finance mystery" but, as you can see, understanding capital requirements, credit terms, costs, financing capabilities, and so on, this does require some study and guidance.

I can see where that kind of complication can affect even the most modest of small businesses. Have you run across any other consistent problem categories?

Yes. A number of beginners, in trying to cut costs, avoid using an accountant or a lawyer in the initial stages. Depending upon the type and size of the venture, this can prove to be more costly than the start-up consultation.

In many new ventures, the owner/manager often puts in everything he or she can raise and then has no surplus dollars or reserves available for any of the difficult times that may occur.

Undercapitalization is not at all unusual in the new small business. It isn't always fatal, but it does take an extra dollop of good management to survive with that handicap.

Of course, start-up situations are quite often deficient in management experience. Without any definitive past history, money is often squandered on a lavish showroom or office setup, and it wasn't vital to the operation. Sometimes more money is put into inventory than is warranted and that ties up capital, creates credit problems with suppliers, and strangles your buying capabilities.

Pre-planning, analyzing where you're going, getting help in non-familiar areas, and acquiring knowledge as quickly as possible in the managerial aspects of running a business . . . these are the musts, if you want to succeed.

Accountant: Karlitz and Karlitz— Dobbs Ferry, N.Y.

From your point of view, why is it important for the beginner, even before the actual start-up, to consult with an accountant?

A professional accountant, especially a CPA, has had the advantage of being involved with many, small businesses. In the course of seeing and dealing with all the problems on an intimate basis, hand-in-hand with the owners, there's been the opportunity to grasp, on an intuitive level, the basic principles that apply to all ventures.

The grocer may know how to price groceries and the carpenter may know how to build structures of wood. The accountant may not know any of these things, but he does know what applies to all businesses. When the small entrepreneur gets this kind of input in the beginning stages, before anything has been done, it can be invaluable. We have many situations where people come in after the fact and ask us, in effect, to "Please take this can of worms and make it into a gourmet's delight."

We recommend, and we find that it's worth the expense, that it be done beforehand. It costs so much more to fix it up later and very often you save money up front by simply not making foolish mistakes, not duplicating work, incorporating when you don't have to or when it's unwise, and not doing any number of just plain wrong things. In addition to that, it puts your mind at rest, knowing that you've sought out and received professional advice.

When the beginners do start, isn't there some simple method of keeping records? Do they have to immediately go into double-entry bookkeeping?

First of all, records are mandatory. The IRS requires them and they are also extremely valuable for the owner/manager to determine where the business is going. The simplest bookkeeping system, incidentally, is an accurate and neat checkbook. This is what should be kept in mind by all beginners. Then, when they do need help and advice, it can be given without any frustrating mental gyrations or costly time-consuming labor. The checkbook stub should be totally descriptive . . . . date, check number, amount, and what the transaction was all about. On the other side of the stub, deposits should be recorded . . . their source and nature . . . whether they're income, loans, or whatever.

From there the entrepreneur can start a double-entry bookkeeping system or use one of the DOME books that are available in your stationery store. I recommend those bookkeeping books to beginners who are on such a small level that they can't afford any type of advice. Although adequate for records, you could make a mistake in them and never know it.

Double-entry bookkeeping is extremely simple, even though it seems complex to those who have never tried it. Strangely enough, some of the "homemade" systems are more difficult, although that wasn't intended. Good business sense dictates that you should use the double-entry system because of the checks and balances that are built in. Once you start with it, the same structure will function no matter how large your company becomes.

This system is even more important when the business is growing and the owner/manager is so busy that he or she is no longer on top of everything. When the owner is there every day and knows every penny that goes in and out, that entrepreneur will usually be aware of what the situation is, at almost any point. Records and financial statement analysis, under those conditions, are not relied upon as much because of the personal control that exists. When the owner, however, becomes one step removed by hiring a bookkeeper or having another party keep the records, then the situation starts to change.

That's where you, the CPA, functions best. Can you elaborate on that?

Books, records and financial statements become extremely important when the business has outgrown the direct control of the small-business entrepreneur. To some degree now, there's a kind of absentee managership that occurs. The bookkeepers can compile data and keep everything up to date but there's no interpretation on their part. From time to time the owner will call upon the bookkeepers for accounting decisions simply because of their proximity, but that can create problems or make things worse than they should be.

From the point of view of checking for material errors, auditing, and financial statement analysis, the CPA's are working on an after-the-facts situation . . . that's an extremely valuable function on their part. But, additionally, there are many management advisory services that we perform before, during, and in after-the-fact situations. Sometimes these are more valuable to the small businessman because they relate to the many ongoing decisions that have to be made for business performance . . . and that can be translated into the factors of survival and future growth.

Accountant/Owner: Marvin Nelson CPA— New York, N.Y.

A beginner often doesn't consult a professional because of the cost involved. Is an initial consultation expensive?

A good professional will not cost a business a penny . . . in more ways than one. If someone has the basic information sketched out and wants me to look it over, that kind of consultation will not be charged.

After reviewing some of those basics, we don't have to make a five-year projection to analyze the situation. We can focus in immediately to the problem areas and if it looks like a bad deal, say, "Don't go into that deal, don't waste your time and money." Even in a surface exploration like that it's possible to come up with some answers, simply because of our very diverse business experience and our first-hand knowledge of the pitfalls that a small business usually involves.

However, when the business does get started, there will be fees. We attempt to minimize these fees until the owner develops the business, the profitability, and the cash flow. At that time we hope to recoup our investment with the company. And we hope that the individuals who are in that business will recognize what we are doing for them.

Any business, whether very small or substantial, should have proper books and records to start off with. They should be designed by a CPA who has familiarity with systems work and who knows how what is initially structured will lead eventually to a computer setup, whether it's an in-house one, or at a service bureau. That's where the future is.

*What about buying a business? That's where an account-
ant seems to be mandatory.*

Buying a business is more difficult than starting one. Essentially, you may
be buying someone else's headache and that's just what you want to avoid.
You want to know why the person is selling the business, what the true
profits are, what is verifiable and what is not. We have to analyze sales, the
profits over a number of years, what the future potential for that particular
industry is, the financial statements and tax returns for five years, et cetera.
Then we make some projections, see where cuts can be made, expenses
lowered, or note any areas of the present operation that may not be desired.
After that, we can make an evaluation.

Don't forget we are offering a recommendation to our client to make a
substantial investment when it involves buying an established business.
Accountants, basically, are conservative people. They want to feel 100
percent sure when they recommend that a business be purchased. All in all,
however, what's most important is the *future potential* of that business. It's
not so much where it's been, but where can it go, that counts.

*Some people say that your functions relate only to what's
past . . . is that a true evaluation?*

No, not at all! At least 50 percent of our work is in the planning area.
Planning for future profits, for *tax* minimization, estate planning, and
things of that nature. It's creative.

Awareness is another area. By translating what has happened in the past
records, we can advise management of some of the problems that lie ahead if
certain steps are not taken. And, there may be the possibility of an
acquisition or merger. Many a small business has desired to take over a
competitor or to diversify. To do so requires not only an evaluation of the
other venture, but also a financial understanding of how it will affect the
original business, the tax consequences, the dilution of commitment, and
the profitability of the total entity. These are all futures!

*Getting back to a start-up operation, why do you think
an accountant should be consulted?*

Because the accountant is—or can be, in a sense—the *director*. He has a
background in taxation, finance, and business management that the aver-

age person starting out in business doesn't have. When the accountant looks at a potential business it's with both the short-range and long-range points of view.

In the short range . . . what are the cash requirements for that business; the owner's personal commitment of capital; sources of other equity; how long will it take to turn the corner; cash flow progression; and what the cash and return expectations would be after the first year. Then, what will they be for longer periods of time?

The form of the business becomes important. We can explain the differences and tax consequences of a sole proprietorship, partnership, Subchapter S corporation, and a corporation. Lawyers would handle the incorporation of a business, we don't. But we would relate the tax laws that apply and then advise the best form for that entrepreneur.

From the start, depending upon the form of business organization that has been chosen, the beginner may also be exposed to the unfamiliar areas of sales tax, resale certificate, employee identification number, federal and state witholding taxes, unemployment taxes, property tax, franchise tax, and other governmental report forms. Some are simple, some are complex. Checking with an accountant beforehand helps one to become aware and it cuts down some of the apprehension, too.

If we don't know enough about the specific business to be started, our thirty years in accounting gives us a wide range of friends in our field who have clients in that business. They would give us the essentials and any of the proficiencies we would need to factor into our projections. After all the initial preparations are undertaken, we would then like to follow through and hold the hand of the new entrepreneur to make sure he continues in the right direction.

Lawyer: Rothfeld and Rothfeld— New York, N.Y.

Is it necessary to consult a lawyer before starting a business?

Perhaps. The first important thing to ascertain, depending upon the type business to be started, is the organization form. Will it be operated as a corporation, or under the owner's name as a trade name . . . which has to be filed in the County Clerk's office. Or, if it's somewhat larger and there are partners involved, will there be partners who are not willing to be personally responsible? If so, the form may have to be a limited partnership, where the only people personally responsible are the general partners. Those who are limited partners have investment but they can't be held responsible if the company goes broke, or is indebted.

When you hold stock in a corporation, the only personal liability you may have is if you fail to pay social security taxes and sales taxes. Then the people handling the money in the corporation are personally responsible because these are trust funds. You are also responsible for labor . . . employees who have not been paid . . . there are serious penalties for that. Other than that, there are no liabilities unless in the course of doing business you not only sign for the corporation but, in addition, you as well as the corporation are responsible. This can be in the case of a bank loan, factoring your accounts receivables, or when you sign a lease while first starting.

What about costs when it comes to incorporating?

The expenses for a corporation run approximately $110. Attorneys who know what they're doing and who have the interests of their clients at heart will charge usually $400 to $500 plus the expenses, to form a corporation. You will see advertisements where attorneys will form a corporation for $250, including expenses. This is the type of work usually done by a paralegal and if you have a client just going into business who needs advice, sometimes weekly or monthly, they're in the wrong stable. There won't be that personal interest involved and maybe not even that expertise to help, when needed. If the beginners do form a corporation, and from time to time have to pick up a phone to find out if they can do this or do that, it's better if they're in the hands of an experienced attorney, who will treat them as if they are part of the office.

Too many people are apprehensive about being charged for every question or phone conversation. This is not true and it's somewhat dependent upon the relationship. In a small or medium-size firm, the client will be treated as one of the family, so to speak. Of course, if he or she is constantly calling, it may be a case of requiring regular and ongoing legal work. Maybe the best thing there is a retainer agreement. Retainers can create their own problems. When they become too burdensome for the attorney, he would want to increase the fee. When there isn't much work, the client begins to wonder whether he's getting his money's worth.

What are some other areas that the beginner may require assistance in . . . legal or otherwise?

There are so many things involved in a lease, for example, that I think they should have an attorney. Do you have the right to assign it, if your business goes down? It may be a good location and someone else may be willing to take it, or you may want to sub-let it. Additionally, there may be a question as to the use the premises may be put to. Many leases restrict how that specific location may be used . . . designing, manufacturing, type of retail store, et cetera. The client needs something to protect his or her own interests. Within the lease, can you get options to renew? Is there a tax escalation clause? Is there a "porterhouse" formula, where you have to pay for increases to labor, fuel, and services?

In a shopping mall, is there a minimum rent and then a percentage of sales formula? How are those sales checked? Will you have the protection of a restriction on competitors to your type of store or something closely allied? In all these cases of premises leases, it will be extremely advantageous to have an attorney negotiate with you or, at the very least, to review what is being offered.

When you have a corporation or partnership, you have a stockholders agreement with the others involved. Provisions have to be made in the event of long-term illness and in case someone wants to step out of the business—how much will the payments be and how will they be paid? If the full amount the withdrawing participant put in were to be taken out, the business might be bankrupt. The same thing applies in the case of death and payment to the estate.

In any event, an agreement beforehand will spell out these details relative to insurance, buy-out, book value, good will, and certificates of evaluation.

Many other things are included in this before-you-start stage . . . who signs checks, equality in salaries, spheres of responsibility, how disputes are resolved, amount of draws . . . and any additional items that could cause dissention when the venture is in actual operation.

As legal counsel to small businesses, you've had the opportunity to become aware of many of their common problems.

Oh, yes. One area that's quite important is good recordkeeping. Keep complete tabs on income and accounts receivable and make sure to follow them up. Watch credit carefully because I've seen credit become a big problem. They want the business so badly that they take credit risks. This is more costly in the long run than no business at all.

It's important to set up a good rapport with a bank, so that the bank will have confidence in you and your business. Since banks can become impersonal, deal with one individual as much as possible.

Watch overhead, because expenses always keep going up. In good times many small businesses don't worry about it. But when things get bad, the overhead is hard to cut back. So always hold back and don't get too liberal.

Legally, as they're operating, there are always questions that come up. Don't hesitate to get in touch before, not after. Once you get into trouble, it's always more costly to get out.

Lawyer: J. Stulberg—Pelham, New York

You are a special counsel to Support Services Alliance, which is a nonprofit organization that assists the small entrepreneur and the self-employed. What are some of the legal problems that arise?

They primarily relate to the payment or non-payment of money from customers or suppliers. Frequently a supplier furnishes goods to be sold by the businessperson and the goods don't sell. The understanding of the businessperson was that the goods could be returned to the supplier for credit, but the supplier didn't view it as a consignment type of arrangement and is demanding full payment. The businessperson calls and calls and gets no response, until one day the response consists of a lawyer's letter requesting payment or a day in court. It can frequently involve a lot of money on goods that are seasonal or trendy.

It also relates, obviously, to being able to make business decisions to determine how much inventory to carry on goods that have a limited sale-life, so as not to be left with a large unsold stock. Often it is possible to work out legal relationships for holding inventory . . . perhaps, on a consignment basis . . . but this idea doesn't seem widespread among the smaller businesses. A quick check with an attorney can often delineate the different kinds of contractual obligations the businessperson is undertaking when they engage in purchasing goods and services.

Another example relates to the delivery of defective goods and refusal to pay. Often there's nothing written that is clear, and discussions don't resolve the problem. Frequently it's a matter of negotiations, being able to effectively negotiate an acceptable solution. The dollar amounts I've encountered in this capacity have not been substantial . . . two or three thousand at the most. But it is a lot of money to the businessperson, and when you look at what the lawyer's fees are to litigate this, you may tend to wipe out whatever you've claimed. So it's important to settle this type affair outside the court. That's one reason why people turn to our agency.

Do these problems relate to that old adage of "make sure everything is in writing?"

Well, there's an interesting conflict here because to some extent the small businessperson has a sense of independence and wants to be able to conduct business with a handshake or the spoken word. Putting it in writing is almost antithetical to that way of doing business. It clearly can have repercussions. I think the challenge is to figure out a way to establish simple documents that are not offensive to anyone reading them. The kind that can be accepted in the course of doing business, not as a defensive posturing by each party, but more as a way of making sure that the relationship is just as clear as possible.

An attorney serves his client best when he knows the nature of the business to such a degree that he can take what he knows about the law and then help draft a series of business procedures that are in compliance with the law but that don't get in the way of the normal flow of doing business.

If a beginner is going to incorporate, consulting a lawyer is an obvious step. Are there any do's and don'ts that relate to the start-up?

The decision to incorporate is not only a business decision, it should also be viewed from a legal context. There are some instances in which it may be premature to incorporate. There are costs involved and it may be a question of when you want to incur those costs. There's the question of what potential liability your business will expose you to and whether you should have the protection an incorporation gives you. Do you want this from the beginning or should the business start as a sole proprietorship and then incorporate down the line somewhere?

If the delayed way is how you start, then what impact will that have on the name you use as a sole proprietor? Will there be a way of preserving that name, once it's established, when you do decide to incorporate?

Other areas that you could call upon an attorney, just in terms of reviewing, would be the strategy in negotiating terms of a lease, employment practices and labor laws, partnership arrangements and employment contracts, and so on, as the business progresses. At best, consulting an attorney will force you to think more clearly about the enterprise you are about to undertake . . . simply because of the questions the attorney will ask. That may be the most important thing that can happen, especially when the decision to go ahead is made and the inevitable legal matters start to pop up.

What about relationships and fees?

People ought to feel free to shop for attorneys. I know it's one thing to say this and another to do it . . . something like shopping for doctors. When you do go to one doctor, there's a sense of being committed. You think you're going behind his back if you try elsewhere. Often, however, a lawyer finds it best to refuse a case and a client does have those same rights. The entrepreneur must look for someone that he or she feels confident of and comfortable with.

In the matter of fees, lawyers are also in business and if a significant amount of time is taken up in consultation or continuing advice, they are entitled to charge. On the other hand, they are there to provide a service to a client. Part of that service is to be available and not to have the person feel that every thirty seconds is going to cost x number of dollars. There are a variety of fee arrangements that are made between attorneys and their clients . . . I don't believe that it's necessarily prohibitive in terms of cost for people to go to attorneys. Securing legal advice at the beginning should be viewed as a cost of doing business and, hopefully, it will be a prudent investment that will save money in the future.

Obviously, there is a limit to the beginner's resources and it's essential for the client to be forthright in asking what the legal advice is going to cost . . . as best as can be projected at that time.

Insurance Broker: Cohen Insurance— New York, N.Y.

How do you feel about consultation with the profession- als before starting a business?

I think there are three people the new entrepreneurs should consult before they start a business . . . an attorney, an accountant, and an insurance broker/agent.

As an example, with reference to the insurance aspect, if you incorporate your business, you immediately need the statuatory coverages. These are workmen's compensation insurance . . . which is required in every state . . . and in New York and several other states you need disability benefits insurance. They are the statutory coverages required by the Department of Labor. Even if you are the only person in the corporation, you are an employee and that insurance is needed.

In the event that you are operating as a partnership or sole proprietorship, the disability insurance is voluntary, but in any case you do need the compensation insurance. Within most states you take out compensation coverage through an insurance agent or broker . . . but there are a number of "monopolistic" states where you must obtain the compensation insurance from the state . . . Ohio, West Virginia, Washington, Arizona.

I know insurance coverage can vary with the type of business. Are there some commonalities?

If we're talking about a retail store, manufacturing company, office, even a service unit, they are all going to be signing a premises lease. The minute you sign, you should have insurance. If there are renovations going on, or furniture and fixtures being installed, or stock and inventory being shelved . . . there may be months elapsing between the signing of the lease and the actual opening for business. During this two or three month period, there are people working on the premises, alterations being done, and maybe a general contractor at work. It's important that you have basic liability coverage. As soon as your name goes on that lease, you need that protection.

If there is a general contractor on the premises, he should give you a certificate of insurance, which gives evidence that he has workmen's compensation and general liability insurance. Otherwise you would be responsible for injury on the premises, even though you had nothing to do with it. Send that certificate to your broker for review. They can check if the limits are adequate, the coverage is adequate, the insurance company is authorized in the state and that it has the facilities to handle claims, if they occur.

Additionally, the retail shop may need plate glass insurance, whereas the manufacturing unit may require boiler or machinery coverage. There are many types of applicable insurance and an experienced agent/broker can guide you initially through these to determine the mandatories, the advisables, and any of the specifics that may only apply to your type of business.

Since the average beginner is not familiar with this area, can he or she come in for an awareness session?

If they are serious about starting a business, most insurance agents or brokers would be glad to give a prospective client a half or one hour of their time without charging a fee. There's a great deal to cover and I think awareness is the right word for it.

The first thing a new entrepreneur should think about are the statutory coverages . . . compensation and disability. Then, immediately, liability insurance to protect the new business, as well as coverage on the premises itself while constructing or renovating. When you have property of value in the premises . . . furniture and fixtures, equipment, stock and inventory . . . you will require property insurance.

Most insurance agents or brokers will acquaint you with all-risk insurance. It covers loss or damage not only from fire and theft, but water damage, vandalism, explosion, civil commotion, riot, or what have you. Today these are all very important aspects.

Another type of coverage that everyone should give some thought to is business interruption insurance. Whether you are in retail, manufacturing, wholesaling, or even in a service venture, this can be extremely important. There have been numerous cases where a new business, a retail store for example, may have had a fire after being open for a short time. The insurance company will give the funds to refurnish the store and replenish the inventory . . . but, during this period, there is no income! The rent and other expenses must still be paid; personnel, if any, would want to be retained on some kind of holding basis, profits become non-existent, et cetera.

The business interruption insurance reimburses you for all the additional expenses incurred during the period of interruption and will also pay you for loss of profits for that time. The cost for this kind of insurance is fairly reasonable . . . it's usually fifty percent of the base fire insurance rate.

I recall phrases like . . . "there's never too much insurance" or "no such thing as enough liability insurance." That kind of thing really unnerves a beginner entrepreneur.

True, but that owner/manager must have protection for the new business. An experienced agent or broker will give guidance based both upon the specific needs of the venture and the vast experience gained from serving others in the same type of business. Without question, affordable costs may be a determining factor in what is finally selected, but an awareness of what is applicable will also have been acquired.

Once a basic insurance program has been initiated, riders or temporary increases can be obtained at a pro-rata basis of the annual rate. This is less expensive than buying coverage, as you need it, without having a yearly package policy. In this way if there's a huge inventory buildup for a month or two, temporary coverage can be increased reasonably. If renovations create a greater liability potential for customers, a rider to increase the basic policy's limits can be similarly handled. The new entrepreneur and his or her insurance advisor can work together to control costs and provide as much protection as possible.

The very fact that all businesses require some sort of insurance and protection is the very reason that a potential entrepreneur should consult an insurance agent or broker before the business starts up.

Insurance Agent: The Goodhart Agency— Yonkers, N.Y.

Let's start with the thought of buying a business. How does the buyer relate that to the insurance aspect?

In some cases, depending on the policies, certain existing insurance can be transferred to the new owner. In other instances some policies must be cancelled and rewritten, particularly if it's a new company taking over the business.

What should be done, however, is the complete schedule of existing insurance—which shows all the policies, their coverages, their costs—must be obtained before the sale is completed. Then your own insurance agent or broker can check over the information to make sure that the coverage was adequate and the costs were in line. Previous insurance costs may have been understated to make the overall figures of the business look better or the former owner may have been omitting some desirable types of coverage in an effort to keep a low overhead.

Another interesting aspect is location. This applies to starting or buying a business, as well as having an established venture move to a new premises. Fire rates should be checked because they vary from building to building. All commercial buildings are rated individually. The rates can be extremely high depending upon where the building is located, its construction, and the type of tenants that are already in that building.

Aside from the compensation, liability, fire and theft, et cetera, what are some coverages the beginning entrepreneur would not usually think of?

Many times a new business will start without the employee and management protection type coverages . . . group insurance, major medical, life insurance, and so on. It's a big consideration that is often overlooked when someone is leaving a job and going into business for themselves. They sort of forget that they had this nice little package of protection at work. It's poor planning to give it up when they start anew. Their idea is to go along for the first year in the new business and then give it some thought later.

But, that's just when someone in the family does get sick. They really should budget that into their plans as a cost of doing business.

An area that never occurs to the uninitiated is products liability coverage. If he or she is manufacturing or wholesaling something that is even slightly out of the ordinary, this type of protection may apply. Products liability rates during the past five years have sometimes gone up five- and ten-fold and it may be quite a shock to find out what the costs will be. If you were manufacturing a small toy, for example, and marketing it . . . this may be seemingly harmless to the entrepreneur, but it doesn't seem the same way to an insurance underwriter. Because of the high rates involved, it may throw the whole business plan out of proportion.

In the case of partnerships, there's a whole range of insurance that can apply. Buy-out insurance is one type that enables the business to buy out the other partner's share in the event of death . . . without using funds from the business itself. When a new venture starts out, costs are being carefully watched, but it is something that—if not taken care of immediately—should be dated ahead so as not to be forgotten.

If there is a mortgage or a loan made . . . and that can apply to a building, property, equipment, contents of a store or warehouse . . . the fire and extended coverage will always be required for at least the amount of the loan. The bank, or lending agency, or lessor, must be named on the policy as mortgagee or loss payee. The loss, if it occurs, is payable first to them. The fire and extended coverage is the least insurance required; it is very possible that more may be requested.

Very often, when someone goes into business, they want to transfer their car to the business or buy one. The rates, of course, will be higher for commercial use than those for personal use. In the case of using a personal car for business, whether it's the owner's or anyone else's who works for the business, there is an endorsement on the general liability policy called an employer's non-ownership liability. With this, even when a personal car is being used, it furnishes protection for the business from any lawsuit that would result from an accident where a personal car was being used for business.

Do you have a check-off list that you and the prospective small-business entrepreneur can work off?

Yes, we do. There are many other fine points and pitfalls in setting up an insurance program and you really have to go to an agent who is thoroughly familiar with commercial insurance. Take the case of a business shipping goods by truck. Very often they think if anything happens, the trucking company is responsible for it. Not necessarily so. It's usually better to have your own transportation policy for the goods you ship.

The point is to discover what is applicable to the particular business and what is affordable to each venture when starting up. A professional agent will give the prospective client a proposal, in writing, as to all the coverages being given, their amounts, and the costs of each type of coverage. Then there will be no question as to what was covered and what was not covered. Additionally, there will be a record of coverages that were recommended, even if they were not purchased at the beginning. Our tickler file will then enable us to alert the client for periodic review and a follow-up for those coverages that were delayed for a later date.

For the purpose of not overlooking anything, the check-off list is quite extensive and contains eight major categories. There will be some duplication of coverages within these categories and often an all-risk or *all-peril* type package will cover most areas. It would be interesting to list them for your readers:

Liability: 22 classifications. From workmen's compensation to umbrella liability.

Buildings: 13 classifications. From fire and extended coverage to plate glass.

Loss to Business Personal Property: 20 classifications. From fire and extended coverage to parcel post.

Loss of Income: Seven classifications. From business interruption to valuable papers.

Boiler and Machinery Loss: Three classifications.

Human Failure: 10 classifications. From blanket position bond to home of messenger.

Employee Protection: Six classifications. From group life to pension.

Management Protection: 10 classifications. From key man insurance to officer and directors E and O.

A total of 91 classifications covering almost everything the insurance companies could think of. Fortunately, for the beginning entrepreneur, the very great majority don't apply. But, all in all, they are in themselves a very good reason for the new owner/manager to consult an insurance agent or broker before he or she starts the venture.

Business Broker: Shadron Realty— Tucson, Arizona

I'm not sure of the exact functions that a business broker performs. Would you explain some of the background?

A business broker has a responsibility both to the buyer and the seller. The first thing we do is try to find out as much as we can about the business that's offered for sale, using our own ratios and performance standards. We will not accept a business we think is extremely overpriced, or if the books cannot be shown to show a profit.

Rather than run a long column of "any and all" businesses for sale, we stick to a few offerings that are quality designated. Occasionally we may be misled by the sellers and in that case an adjustment must be made.

How and when would that be determined? After the sale takes place?

Oh, no. When "earnest money" is put down, the books and everything else necessary are open to the buyer. His accountant and lawyer can check out and analyze all the factors before the sale is finalized.

In our method of selling, when we write a contract, we give the buyer ten days or two weeks to qualify the business. Within that time he has the right to back out and take his "earnest money" with him should anything be not as stated by the owner.

That "earnest money" is necessary as a preliminary to examining the books and records . . . how much is usually involved?

Yes, otherwise anyone could come in off the street and say they want to look over the books . . . it could be his competitors or just curiosity-seekers. The "earnest money" is part of an actual sales contract . . . it shows a definite desire to purchase, subject to verification of the facts as presented. Usually we are talking about 10 percent, but it can vary, depending upon circumstances.

You indicated that you qualify the seller somewhat. How about the buyer?

We can't force the buyers to bring in their bank statements, but we do emphasize that there's no use in wasting each other's time if they don't have the resources called for by a particular offering. It's necessary to match their downpayment ability and their need for returns with the size of the business that can accomodate these two factors. The eventual income is usually proportional to the investment that's made.

At the same time, if the buyer has $50,000 to invest, we try to relate to a smaller down payment, so that he has ten or fifteen thousand for working capital. Of course, this is all dependent upon the business that is chosen and whether income is immediate or not.

Additionally, it's extremely important for us to have a strong interest in the future success of the buyer. If we sell a business that isn't right for the person, it will come back to haunt the both of us. We want him to succeed . . . that's why I visit each business I've sold within two or three months after the sale to see how everything is going along.

Although you are not impartial, is it honestly better to buy a business rather than start from scratch?

I've got to say yes for a number of reasons. If you do buy an established business, you can take money home the first month or year that you're in operation. Conversely, when starting a business, you will generally have to feed that venture for the first year or year and a half. You may also require additional capital over and above your initial investment . . . more so than for a business that already has clientele coming through the door.

Also, another point. To start a business, you have to buy furniture and fixtures, equipment and inventory. That inventory is, almost without exception, a cash outlay, because no supplier is going to give credit without a track record. Equipment, on the other hand, may involve financing terms.

Let's take the initial investment factor. If the seller has been making a profit in his business, he will usually not take more than 29 percent down . . . the other 71 percent will be carried back by him in a contract, with terms. This type of deal benefits him taxwise and there, hopefully, we may also see a number of positives for the buyer.

He or she is basically starting a business with only a 29 percent initial investment . . . a lot less, perhaps, than buying everything that's required when you go from scratch. There's no need to go to the bank for a loan because, in effect, the seller is making the loan. Because the seller is carrying back that other 70 percent, the odds are good that he will also be more realistic with his sales price.

Additionally, given that financing structure, I imagine the seller would be very interested in rooting for the buyer.

No question about that . . . it is to the seller's benefit also. Incidentally, we do require that all of our sellers stay for a specific length of time, depending upon the nature of the business. This can involve training, employee rapport, introduction to clients and suppliers . . . everything to facilitate a smooth transition. It's of no value to the seller to see that business, with the new owner, go downhill. Then he may have to take it back and try to sell it again . . . in its lowered state. Or, with a lot of effort, take the time to build it back up again. That's not a happy situation.

Suppose your prospective buyer has no specific skill or past owner/manager experience? He or she may have some business sense and knowledge, but not in running a business. Can that type of person succeed?

If they apply themselves diligently, yes. Especially if they go into an established business . . . where the books are already set up, the buying schedule is set up, the personnel and salary scales exist, the pricing policy and suppliers are established, and the selling market area is already identified.

Looking at the books to confirm that all these factors are working well, offers a successful, established pattern to follow. Then a person with average intelligence with some training, plus a strong commitment to learn on-the-job . . . this person can succeed. When you start from scratch, however, you had better know what you are doing or else have a great deal of luck.

> *Suppose the business for sale doesn't have a great profit picture, but still looks somewhat desirable . . . is that worth pursuing?*

Well, if you get a business like that before it's gone downhill too far . . . because of poor management, inexperience, or lack of capital . . . it requires a buyer who knows that type of business and realizes exactly what's wrong with it. That buyer understands the operation can be turned around to make it go toward a more profitable picture.

To sell this kind of business to someone who has not been in business before, you'll be putting that buyer into bankruptcy within sixty days.

Business Broker/Owner—The Drescher Agency, Inc.—Spring Valley, N.Y.

> *Although you represent the seller, what benefits or protection do you offer the buyer?*

When we list a business, we make our ads very extensive, so that we give as much information as possible. This may include: type of business, hours, gross sales, net returns, lease details, down payment and/or price, and future potential. This is an ad, perhaps in *The New York Times,* that can run anywhere from $100 to $500.

We don't want 100 calls on that ad. We would rather have three or four and sell one of those potentials. When they respond by phone, we suggest they ask any question that is not in the ad. If they are still interested, they are to come to our office for an interview and to fill out a fact sheet.

Basically, it's to *qualify* and guide the buyer. Recently, for example, we had a bakery for sale. A man, who may have been a salesman and never worked with his hands, will come in. He's read the ad and is interested in the idea of netting $1,000 a week. Any question will be answered, but I'm forced to tell him that this is seven days a week; he must get up at 5:00 AM every morning; it's a family-run affair and it's a strenuous job. If he remains interested, he can see it, but I would strongly recommend that he go into another business entirely.

Selectivity and matching certainly make sense. Are there any other areas that apply?

Yes. That ad I mentioned is always attached to and made part of a binder agreement. We try as much as possible to guarantee that what is in the ad, is in the offered business. The binder stipulates that the agreement is subject to the business doing what we advertised. If the accountants and lawyers don't find this to be so, then the deal is off and the binder is returned. Incidentally, that binder, usually for a thousand dollars or so, is made out to our company and held in the file, not deposited until everything is okay. This is needed to temporarily take it off the market . . . it protects the buyer and gives the seller a rationale for opening his books.

Another suggestion we try to have the buyer follow, is that he or she sit in the offered store for two or three weeks. See what's coming across the register, see the operation in action, and then tie the whole thing together.

We also talk to the buyer about potential. A person who is willing to work hard can make a lot of money by being in their own business, if that potential exists. Now there are two ways for the potential to be there . . . either it's inherent in the existing business or it will be so because of the new buyer. That buyer may be "the new broom that sweeps clean" . . . the one who revitalizes the situation with advertising, marketing, or just being there all the way . . . whatever it takes.

The old owner in many, many instances becomes satisfied with what he's been doing, even though it can be improved. He may have worked for twenty or thirty years and the challenge has mellowed. So the possibility of tremendous growth is dependent upon the new buyer. And we have to stress that he has to work his business; if it's absentee ownership, forget about it or be prepared to take the consequences.

Something else I also try to recommend is that the contract, not the binder, stipulate that the previous owner, if possible, will stay there for two, three, or four months at a small stipend salary. An example is the body-shop owner who is staying with the new buyer for a while, on salary, and then will go into adjusting for an insurance company. This one will be a healthy transition situation.

Is there any validity to the advantages of buying a business rather than starting from scratch?

We say that it's similar to buying a new house versus a used one. There's no question about the advantages of a used home . . . storms, screens, finished basement, landscaping, different improvements, a pool . . . things for which the owner never gets his money back. Insofar as a business is concerned, if it shapes up properly, there is also no question that buying an established one is more advantageous.

But you must consider the hidden factor called "key money" . . . good will money. How much is an individual willing to pay for that? That's where we want to come in . . . we try to relate to the buyer getting back his original investment in about a *year*. If the present owner is netting around a thousand dollars a week, we want to keep the down payment to fifty thousand or less, no matter what the sales price is. Of course, there are certain exceptions but that is the rule I try to follow.

We've been here twenty years, operating only in Rockland county . . . we're very familiar with all aspects of business in the area and we feel we're quite capable in sizing up an individual and a business. I'm very, very active in the community and our company enjoys a fine reputation. That's important to both buyer and seller. We're here to stay and we're involved with the community's health and growth, especially its business environment.

11 Getting It All Together

Starting a small business of your own is the culmination of getting it all together . . . the initial drive, the preparation, the risks.

Winning is keeping it all together . . . the enthusiasm, the perseverance, the "quick learn," a touch of luck.

For starters, you have to get past the master checklist . . . that's a review of preparation. If you don't make it, think twice before you go ahead.

What you've read thus far should have filled in some of the blank spaces. It's only the beginning. Continue acquiring awareness from as many sources as possible, so that the "gamble" is a calculated risk . . . not a wish and a prayer.

THE ENTREPRENEUR'S "GO FOR IT" CHECKLIST

As initially indicated, preparation is mandatory for anyone who wishes to start and manage his or her own small business.

Being prepared, however, doesn't mean becoming an accomplished owner/manager overnight. Most of the eventual expertise acquired by a successful entrepreneur is usually the result of a starting basic knowledge and motivation, plus the learning derived from actually running a business.

When the entrepreneurial spirit does hit you, it is vital to develop an awareness of what lies ahead . . . for it can often cushion the jolting realities that abound in this high-risk field. Part of that awareness can come from reading books about small business; attending relevant business courses and seminars; studying case histories and talking with other entrepreneurs; checking out government aids, trade associations and industry publications.

Additionally, thinking it out beforehand is one of the keys to evaluating the probability of success. Toward that aspect, a review of the following checklists may help indicate the advisability of going into your own business or, perhaps, forgetting the whole idea.

191

Personal Characteristics

Some of the questions in these overall checklists may not apply to every individual or to every proposed business. But a review of personal characteristics is the one area that does apply to everyone.

An honest self-appraisal is one of the first essential steps towards entrepreneurship. On the other hand, it may trigger the realization that running a business is really not something you hankered for, after all. Incidentally, the questions don't require a flat yes or no . . . it's better to evaluate yourself by percentage or degree.

- Is your energy level above average? Your health good?

- Are you willing to work harder than ever before?

- Can you self-start without direction from others?

- Do you get discouraged easily?

- Do you absorb new experiences rapidly?

- Can you cope with responsibility . . . total responsibility?

- Are you confident about making decisions . . . quickly, if necessary, and with some degree of accuracy?

- Are you able to get along well with people?

- Can you motivate others . . . employees?

- What about risks . . . have you usually played it safe? Are you reluctant to take chances?

- Can you analyze situations fairly well?

- Have you carefully checked out your motivation and determination . . . the why's of your decision for self employment?

Type of Business

The real "pro" in business is the one who doesn't worry about what specific business to choose. It's the challenge of a profit-making situation that counts. He or she relates to the "business of business" and can adapt energy and knowledge to any project.

Most new entrepreneurs, however, are dependent upon a particular skill, a professional experience, a recent position, some specific studies, or a unique idea.

- Have you thought of a business you wish to start?

- Will you be a manufacturer, distributor, wholesaler, retailer, or services supplier?

- Is it based upon your present skills or work experience?

- Does it reflect a hobby or specific interest?

- Do you have broad, all-around experience in this field . . . or expertise in only one area?

- Is it better to get more knowledge by working for someone else in this field?

- Will you need a partner with additional skills that can complement your own?

- Is there a need for your proposed product or service?

- Does your idea have a marketable advantage over existing situations?

- Have you identified your total market; categories of buyers; your suppliers?

- If a product is involved, how will it be distributed?

- Have you initially researched the field . . . checked competition; growth potential; business conditions; trade sources; general areas of location?

- Do you think your idea can be profitable in relation to the money and time that will be needed?

- Have you discussed your plans with a knowledgeable, experienced advisor?

Before You Start

As you work your way through motivation, enthusiasm, preliminary investigation, and almost-final determination . . . there are still many more steps to probe and finalize. Rather than viewing them as road blocks, think positive and consider them as additional "votes of confidence" . . . especially if you have already tackled them.

- Have you evaluated the various ways to start your entrepreneurship?

> buy an existing business
> become a franchisor
> start your own business from scratch
> begin on a part-time basis

- Do you know the advantages and disadvantages of each type start-up situation?

- What about the financial aspect . . . did you try to map out your initial dollar needs?

> furniture and fixtures
> equipment requirements
> inventory
> working capital
> salaries—if any
> rent, utilities, insurance
> professional fees, licenses

- Did you research the industry, trade associations, wholesalers, et cetera, to realistically estimate your initial sales volume?

- Have you tried to evaluate a number of competitors in this field? . . . their pro's and con's?

- Which type of business organization did you decide to form?

> sole proprietorship
> partnership
> corporation
> subchapter S

- Have you taken the time to write out a very simple business plan? One that just outlines:

> what you intend to do
> why you are doing it

whether you work alone or with others
where you will obtain your initial capital
how much capital is required to start
why your product or service is better
who or what constitutes your market
how you relate to your competitors
where you will get your inventory or supplies
your general methods of procedure
your projected sales
your first year's targets

- Does there appear to be a sound economic relationship between investment and anticipated sales . . . i.e., the estimated cost of goods and general expenses subtracted from the estimated projection of sales?

- Have you surveyed the typical operating ratios for your type business? . . . Dun and Bradstreet, National Cash Register, Trade Associations, et cetera?

- Does this type of business require special licenses, permits, or zoning variances? Will it be subject to Federal regulations?

Financing

Start-up loans for a *new* business are extremely difficult . . . almost impossible . . . to obtain from a commercial bank or the Small Business Administration, especially if you have no previous track record as an owner/manager. Much has been written about the positive loan potential that exists in the SBA and elsewhere, but actualities seem to indicate otherwise. If you do have managerial experience in the field, some capital or collateral of your own, a well-thought-out plan for your proposed project . . . then it is advisable to consult a commercial bank and the SBA.

- Do you intend to use your own savings?

- Will you try to raise money from friends and relatives? From a second mortgage or insurance loan?

- Can a personal loan from your bank or savings and loan association be sufficient for the initial start-up requirements?

- Do you require one or more partners with investment capital?

- If you are going to approach a commercial bank or the SBA, are you familiar with the extensive documentation required for a loan request?

  personal resume
  financial resume
  credit references
  a business plan

- Have you checked whether your personal savings can be used as passbook collateral for a business loan?

- Are you a member of a credit union . . . another possible source of loans?

- For the first year or so, do you have an outside source of income to supplement the initial zero or minimal salary from the business?

Although a start-up loan is difficult to obtain from a commercial bank, it is still advisable for the potential entrepreneur to discuss financing with the professional banker. Even if a loan is not possible, the banker may be able to give you meaningful guidelines for establishing a future credit line, as well as sources of business data that will prove invaluable to your specific project. At the same time you will be impressing him with your research attitude and follow-through.

Starting Out

If you are determined to "go for it" in your own small business, let's double-check some of the previous steps *plus* all the other necessary ones that are vital at this stage. Here again, some facets will not be relevant to your chosen project, but all are worthy of review. In addition to your previous skills and experience, it will be the preparation and completion of these aspects that will make you a successful entrepreneur.

To actually begin operations, have you checked and accomplished *all* of the following:

- Selected the type of business: retail, manufacture, wholesale, distribution, or services?

- Decided on how to start it: buy, franchise, part-time, or start from scratch? Alone or with partners?

- Chosen its structure: sole proprietorship, partnership, corporation?

- Prepared a simple business plan with an economic projection?

- Arranged the financing? Sufficient for six months?

- Selected a business name? Registered it?

- Set up a separate business checking account?

- Consulted a lawyer to handle the legal needs?

- Picked a suitable location: suburban, shopping center, city, heavy traffic area, or off the beaten path?

- Negotiated a lease? Store, office, building?

- Arranged for furniture and fixtures . . . remodeling, if necessary?

- Obtained all necessary licenses and permits?

- Ordered all the utilities? Security systems?

- Purchased stationary, business cards, order forms and invoices?

- Consulted an accountant and insurance broker?

- Set up an initial bookkeeping system and insurance coverage?

- Obtained an employer identification number?

- Arranged for immediate cash requirements as indicated on your previous projections of sales, costs, cash flow and fixed expenses?

- Ordered and set up inventory, equipment and/or supplies?

- Established terms of credit with suppliers?

- Determined operational policies regarding: credit, markups, inventory control, and personnel?

- Set up distribution system . . . retail, direct mail, wholesale or distributors?

- Initiated the opening promotional and advertising campaigns . . . as determined by your identification of customers and market areas.

- Become totally aware of your business objectives; your specific industry; the trade associations; your supply sources; the local competition; the present business conditions and the specific characteristics of your consumers and/or market?

If you've gotten all of the above together, then polish up the last few details and open for business!

Women and the SBA

At one time the Small Business Administration noted in reference to its very extensive services for those who wished to start their own business . . . "There is no program specifically designated *only* for women, nor is there any program denied to women."

As more and more women entered the entrepreneurial field, however, there has been a greater emphasis in that direction. When President Carter established the Interagency Task Force on Women Business Owners, he stated " . . . that as consumers, investors, and workers, women play a vital role in the nation's economy. However, the number and size of women-owned businesses remain remarkably small."

In mid-1979, some of the Task Force's recommendations were implemented and, as a result, certain new commitments were formulated. *Enterprising Women,* a monthly business magazine for women entrepreneurs, reported the following highlights:

- President Carter signed an executive order appointing representatives from 30 Federal Agencies and the White House itself to "promote, coordinate, and monitor activities and plans of the Executive Branch to contribute to the preservation, development and strengthening of women's business enterprises."

- The Small Business Administration (SBA) is targeting $50 million in direct loans to women business owners in 1980, and

initiating a pilot-loan program for women whose needs for starting or expanding a business are for amounts under $20,000.

• The Office of Federal Procurement Policy agreed to pump at least
  $150 million in Federal prime contracts to women-owned firms
  in 1980, and increase that figure to $300 million in 1981. The
  Procurement Office is also issuing government-wide regulations
  to assure that Federal prime contractors increase their use of
  women-owned firms as contractors.

• The Census Bureau was directed to update its 1972 data on
  women-owned companies.

The Department of Commerce, HEW, and many other agencies
began implementing additional programs and commitments in 1980,
through their representation on the Interagency Committee on Women's
Business Enterprise.

The SBA's ongoing training programs and seminars, specifically
targeted for women entrepreneurs, will be continued and enhanced in the
areas of financial assistance, management assistance, and procurement
assistance. A 16-page pamphlet from the SBA, *Women's Handbook—How
SBA Can Help You Go Into Business,* is a must for women who want to start
their own business. It is also meaningful for those who are already in
business and are running into problems, as well as for successful women
business owners who wish to expand their ventures.

The pamphlet is an overview of the SBA services available to women
entrepreneurs, outlining the financial, management, and procurement
programs. It includes a self-evaluation questionnaire, basic business advice,
a guide for loan applications, simple banking terms, and some down-to-
earth starter steps.

For a copy of *Women's Handbook* write: The Small Business Administration, P.O. Box 15434, Fort Worth, Texas, 76119, or call toll free (800)
433–7212. Texas residents, call (800) 792–8901.

To follow up on the assistance you can obtain from the SBA, it is
advisable to check your local phone directory, under U.S. Government, for
the address and phone number of the SBA office in your area . . . if one
exists. Offices are located in 96 cities in the 50 states, and in both Puerto
Rico and Guam.

Statistics in 1977 indicated that women constitute some 52 percent of
the total population, but they only owned 4.6 percent of the nation's
businesses. Their interest in owning and managing businesses is growing
and they are going to SBA for aid in ever-increasing numbers. SBA business
loans approved for women grew from approximately 3,000 loans ($168

million) in fiscal year 1976 to 5,700 loans ($444 million) in fiscal year
1978.

In the same period the number of women counseled rose from 13,500
to 55,500. The number taking SBA-sponsored management-training
courses increased from 49,500 to 122,100.

Since the only available statistics on women-owned businesses dates
from the Bureau of Census survey in 1972, the Task Force conducted much
of its research in areas other than pure numbers . . . the problems,
discriminations, definition, and application of present federal programs, as
they applied to potential and existing women-owned businesses. It was no
surprise to find evidence of obstacles to women who want to enter the
entrepreneurial ranks. The barriers involved sexism, racism, lack of education in relation to nontraditional careers, capital discrimination, and in-
adequate preparation for business.

What is important were some of the specific recommendations made
by the Task Force with relation to the Small Business Administration and
women business owners. A number of them have already been implemented.

- The SBA should be designated as the lead agency in developing
  women's business enterprise in conjunction with other agencies
  and departments.

- The SBA should improve its loan program to women business
  owners . . . by providing incentives to participating banks to
  expand their small loans in order to reach women business-
  owners.

- By training, recruiting, and appointing SBA bank relation of-
  ficers, particularly non-minority and minority women to interact
  with participation in loan guarantee programs.

- Owners of Small Business Investment Companies (SBICS) should
  be urged to invest in women-owned businesses.

- Legislation should be supported by the President to restructure
  SBA's small-business investment companies so they can provide
  more high-risk venture capital into small businesses.

- The SBA should establish management assistance to women
  business owners as a priority and to accomplish this by:

  > Increasing both the number of, and quality of, SBA
  > personnel providing management training to women
  > owners.

Focusing on the special needs and concerns of minority
women.
Increasing substantially the management-assistance program of the SBA.
Improving the SBA's management-information system to
service its clients.

All in all, although most of the problems of small business ownership
apply to *all* business owners, the special federal assistances now developed
for the woman entrepreneur will go a long way toward increasing the
chances for women to enter and survive the small business owner/manager
field.

To facilitate a common understanding and acceptance of what constitutes a woman-owned business, it was necessary for the Task Force to adopt
a definition for data collection and procurement purposes:

- A woman-owned business is a business that is at least 51 percent
  owned, controlled, and operated by a woman or group of women.
  Controlled is defined as exercising the power to make policy
  decisions. Operated is defined as being actively involved in the
  day-to-day management.

Minority Aid—The New Direction

Effective October 1, 1979, the Office of Minority Business Enterprise
(OMBE) was redesignated as the Minority Business Development Agency
(MBDA).

As indicated by the Director of MBDA, the reorganization was not
simply the shifting of boxes on an organizational chart nor only a name
change. It was aimed at refocusing financial and technical assistance to
minority businesses with an eye toward reshaping the overall American
economy—providing more jobs and a better business environment for
minorities.

Two important factors led to the establishment of the Department of
Commerce's new Minority Business Development Agency:

- The perception that Federal minority business development programs have not adequately responded to all minoritiy enterprise

needs, especially in the areas of capital assistance, management and entrepreneurial skills, and data collection.

- The conclusion that rapid acceleration of minorities to increase their ownership, control and management of business assets requires innovative measures to develop medium-sized, job-creating minority firms.

The purpose of the reorganization was to seek a more equitable distribution of business ownership and to cultivate larger, more profitable minority businesses.

What does all this mean to the minority business that requires assistance and to the minority individual who wishes to start a business? It does have a great affect over both. Because MBDA has so many demands on its limited resources, the new direction means that priorities must be established to determine who will receive long-term assistance.

Existing businesses will be accepted as clients only if they meet the following criteria:

- They already have an annual sales volume of $150,000 and/or have five paid employees.

OR

- There is reasonable likelihood that they will reach $150,000 in annual sales and/or have five paid employees within 12 months after MBDA assistance is rendered.

Prospective entrepreneurs (those seeking to start a new business) will be accepted as clients only if their business plans and projections indicate a reasonable likelihood that their ventures will reach an annual sales volume of $150,000, and/or will have five paid employees within two years after MBDA assistance is first rendered.

In effect this also means that all beginners desiring to participate in an MBDA ongoing assistance program must have some sort of business plan that indicates all the ingredients of their proposed business operation.

Additionally, all existing qualified ventures applying for assistance must furnish all the required business and financial information, so that the proper and effective assistance can be supplied to them. If this vital data is not furnished, they will not be helped.

The initial screening of prospective clients is now more thorough than it was in the past. But any minority entrepreneur or prospective owner/manager can still obtain general information or counseling and referral services in all the MBDA-funded organization offices. The priorities previously outlined relates to those clients who require a substantial investment of time by the assisting organization.

In fact, for the accepted and qualified client, the intention is to provide follow-through management and technical assistance for a period of approximately three years after entering the system. This kind of program will go a long way toward encouraging and helping to realize the potential of establishing larger and more profitable minority businesses.

In line with that objective, minority firms will be encouraged to enter the growth industries arena, where the opportunities are better than average for growth and profit. Among these are high-technology firms, health services, communications, safety and security, energy, export-import, wholesale, and transportation.

If you're starting a business or are already established and feel you can qualify for assistance . . . check to see if one of the 270 MBDA-supported business development organizations is in your area. Look in your phone book under U.S. Governnment/Department of Commerce for an OMBE or MBDA listing or ask the Department of Commerce office for this information.

Support Services Alliance

One of the all-important drawbacks of operating a one or two-member small business is the inability to obtain group health or life insurance programs. In factual terms, this would mean getting these necessary benefits at the more reasonable rates enjoyed by the large corporations. Although a number of insurance companies have finally come up with plans that cover two people as the minimum group, the cost advantages are not the same.

A few years ago, with substantial support from the Rockefeller Foundation, Support Services Alliance, Inc., was formed to provide the self-employed and the small organization access to low-cost group services. SSA is a nonprofit organization . . . it has no dues and you can enroll as a member for a fee of only ten dollars.

Among the present group contract and other services available to SSA members are:

- **Insurance:** Comprehensive coverage including life, dental, and long and short term disability insurance at group rates. In most cases, no physical exam is required.

- **Pricing/Purchasing:** Professional buyers are available on a fee basis to give SSA members a target price to negotiate for when making a major purchase or to buy an item not available locally. Special cooperative buying arrangements may be available on a regional basis through SSA chapters.

- **Legal Inquiry and Referral:** SSA members who wish a consultation on a perceived legal problem may have a screening review by telephone for a small fee. An experienced attorney will advise whether or not the problem warrants legal services. If not, he will try to suggest steps the member can undertake on his or her own. If an attorney is needed and the member requires a referral, one is made to the nearest legal referral service in the member's home state.

- **Rentals:** SSA members can participate in the Xerox Contract Pricing Plan, where rental savings, depending on model and volume, can be as high as 15 percent. Hertz cars can also be rented at substantial discounts.

- **Educational Loan Guarantees:** By special arrangement, United Student Aid Funds, Inc. will guarantee college tuition loans made by banks to eligible children of SSA members.

As one example of the kind of coverage the large organizations enjoy, the following comprehensive package is one you can obtain through SSA. This applies to all those who are self-employed or who run a small business.

- The life insurance, underwritten by a group of four major insurance carriers, provides benefits based on earnings or job classifications to a maximum of $100,000. Several options are available.

- The health insurance is administered by Blue Cross/Blue Shield and underwritten by Health Service, Inc., a company wholly owned by the Blue Cross Association. The program includes a basic hospital plan covering semi-private room, board, and ancillary services in full for 365 days; a basic Surgical and In-Hospital Medical Plan; and a Major Medical Plan with $100 deductible and individual lifetime maximum benefits of $1 million over the basic coverages. Persons eligible for Medicare receive the same benefits less the charges covered by Medicare Parts A and B.

There are many other areas that SSA covers in supplying support services to its members. It is becoming a vigorous spokesman in attempting to obtain relief from the burden of government regulations and reporting requirements that apply to small organizations and those self-employed. Also, the need for better access to government contracts and more equitable treatment under the income tax laws is being worked on.

In the matter of information, Skill Series Booklets are being made available on such subjects as: *How To Close Sales, How To Handle Complaints, How To Negotiate, How To Price Products or Services* ($2.75 each).

Also available is a bimonthly Bulletin with 16 pages of practical tips, news and tax briefs, problem solving examples, case histories and other materials of importance to members.

Chapters of SSA, now being formed in community colleges and elsewhere, will provide access to courses, seminars, credit unions and local volunteer attorneys under the Productivity Legal Defense Project.

For membership and/or additional information write:

> Support Services Alliance, Inc.
> Two Times Square
> New York, NY   10036   (212) 398-7800

The varied enrollment options are as follows:

- Basic membership providing access to services; a one-time enrollment fee, but no dues or annual changes $10.00

- Basic membership as above plus a one-year subscription to the SSA Bulletin $16.00

- Participating membership for one year in support of the SSA Productivity Legal Defense Project, including a one-year subscription to the SSA Bulletin $24.00

- If you are already a basic (or chapter) member—a one-year subscription to the SSA Bulletin. $6.00

Many associations of varied self-employed groups and small businesses have spread the word about the benefits derived from SSA. For those who do become members, the best of both worlds can be achieved . . . retaining independence while, at the same time, joining together in a formidable force to gain the bargaining strength needed to garner the same benefits enjoyed by the large corporations.

Sources

In today's real world, the information explosion has just about touched everyone, in every conceivable area. Informed research will inevitably uncover some knowledge concerning any subject under the sun . . . most of it current and all of it helpful, in varying degrees, to the first-time explorer.

If you've never had a small business of your own and wish to become an entrepreneur, you should initially adopt the mantle of an explorer. For, in this instance, that's who you really are . . . searching, learning, checking . . . trying to find your way through a maze of unfamiliar, often intimidating environments.

Fortunately, there's plenty of help available. Too often, however, it's not taken advantage of beforehand. And that is one of the keys that can lead to a successful ownership of your own business. Do a lot of research before you start . . . don't blunder about like the proverbial bull in the china shop, charging up one aisle, then another, causing destruction along the way and finally winding up in a dead-end.

The challenge is to start making that unknown environment of entrepreneurship somewhat more familiar. Try the same approach you've used when buying a new car. That's an area you know something about and still there's a lot of investigating before you put down the money. The competitive ads, magazine articles, manufacturer's brochures, all are perused thoroughly, and a showroom visit is a must. Checking with other owners takes place and if that's okay, you visit a number of dealers to compare prices and service reputations. Finally there's the last review of pro's and con's . . . is a new car necessary; will the old one last a bit longer; will a loan be needed; will the insurance go up too much; what's the mileage comparison?

Since going into your own business is a hundredfold more complex than selecting a new car, the message is obvious. Aside from the very helpful sources like the various government agencies, other entrepreneurs, trade associations, community college courses, seminars, and the professional advisors, there is the big, mandatory must . . . *reading*! Your public library and the local bookstore are two targets to zero in on if you want to get the first smatterings of what entrepreneurship entails. Add to that the hundreds of pamphlets and booklets put out by the Small Business Administration and suddenly the pro's and con's of a small business of your own start to take shape. No, reading, by itself, won't be the end-all and it won't make the go, no-go, decision for you. But it will alert you to the basics, introduce you to the complexities, and above all enable you to decide upon an initial direction . . . toward more specific research.

The other real benefit that comes from an early perusal of small-business books is an understanding of what additional information you need to make your potential idea a reality. If you then talk to a lawyer, the SBA, or another entrepreneur, you will know what questions to ask and what answers you require. The rifle approach of informed research, not the shotgun blast of spattered data . . . there's the payoff. Admittedly, there are many books that can be useful to a beginner, as well as to the new entrepreneur still willing to acquire more assistance in the quest for success. A check of Bowker's *Subject Guide to Books in Print* at the library revealed quite a long listing under the heading of Small Business. A sampling of some recent titles are as follows:

How To Organize and Operate a Small Business by Clifford Baumbach and Kenneth Lawyer. 6th edition. Prentice-Hall.

How To Pick the Right Small Business Opportunity: The Key to Success in Your Own Business by Kenneth Albert. McGraw-Hill.

How To Start and Succeed in a Business of Your Own by John R. Taylor. Reston.

How To Succeed in Your Own Business by William R. Park and Sue Chapin-Park. Wiley.

Small Business: Look Before You Leap by Louis Mucciolo. Arco.

A few of the older titles include:

The Complete Handbook of How To Start and Run a Money-Making Business in Your Home by Marian B. Hammer. Parker.

How To Start and Manage Your Own Small Business by Gardner C. Greene. McGraw-Hill.

Up Your Own Organization by Donald M. Dible. Hawthorne.

Then, there were some others on the library shelves:

How To Start and Operate a Mail-Order Business by Julian L. Simon. McGraw-Hill.

Small-Time Operator: How To Start Your Own Small Business, Keep Your Books, Pay Your Taxes and Stay Out of Trouble by Bernard Kamaroff. Bell Springs.

Successful Small Business Management by Leon A. Wortman. Amacom.

The above listings are only a small fraction of the available titles in this field. Additionally, as indicated, the Small Business Administration publishes a great number of booklets that are concise, easy to understand, and inexpensive. They can be purchased through: Superintendent of Documents, U.S. Government Printing Office, Washington, DC, 20402, or any government bookstore in various large cities.

Check the nearest SBA office for Form SBA 115-B, which lists the booklet titles, number of pages, description, and prices. These are the for-sale publications that can only be purchased from the U.S. Government Printing Office.

There's a large list of *free* pamphlets available from the SBA and they are listed on Form SBA-115A. Copies of these publications can be ordered from:

> Small Business Administration
> P.O. Box 15434
> Fort Worth, Texas   76119

or by toll-free phone: 800–433–7212—(Texas only) 800–792–8901.